ROMAN
FRANCE

ROMAN FRANCE

Paul MacKendrick

St. Martin's Press   New York

To Sal, With Love

Foreword

This book is the fruit of a lifelong love-affair with France, which began forty-three years ago in Taunton, Massachusetts, in affection for a beloved teacher, Florence Mary Kelley; was intensified when I stepped off the boat-train from Dieppe into the Gare St.-Lazare in 1936; and has continued unabated to the present. My daughter, to whom the book is dedicated, remembers—I hope fondly—our fifth-floor walk-up in the Place du Panthéon, on the very site of the Forum of Roman Paris; our sailing toy boats in the pool of the Luxembourg Gardens; the artichokes as big as her head in the restaurant near Les Halles, those splendid Roman basilicas in wrought iron, now, alas, doomed to destruction. My affection for Paris has gone particularly into the last chapter, where I argue *con amore* that it is creative imitation of Roman architecture that has made Paris the most beautiful city in the world.

But France is more than Paris, as the Romans knew, and as any Frenchman living beyond the bounds of the Ile de Paris will passionately attest. And so the book is full, too, of fond memories: of the Dordogne valley, that "golf course of the gods", as one of my students has called it; of Alésia, where the pursuit of Caesar's siegeworks was pleasantly combined with enjoyment of the food and wines of the Côte-d'Or; of the sun-gilded Roman stones of Provence, inextricably blended in my mind with the faint and delicious odor of garlic and the bouquet of Hermitage; of Vaison-la-Romaine, where one has among the ruins the sensation of walking the streets of a live city; of Reims, where one can savor one's half-bottle of Piper-Heidsieck within eyeshot of the Roman Porte de Mars; of St.-Germain-en-Laye, where Roman artifacts are displayed in the palace where James II sighed out his last days in exile; of Orléans, visited for the lively Roman bronzes from Neuvy-en-Sullias, but remembered also because the châteaux are so vivid a Renaissance version of what the prosperous villa-dwellers of

Roman France thought of as the Good Life. In short, the book is the loving record of a pilgrimage in which piety was blended, I hope in due proportion, with *la gourmadise,* surely the most venial of the *péchés mortels.* I hope the reader will enjoy the end product as much as I enjoyed the preliminaries.

Roman France is the fifth in a series (following *The Mute, Greek,* and *Iberian Stones Speak,* and *Romans on the Rhine*), in which I have tried to use archaeological evidence to write cultural history.

The book could not have been written without the kindness of Professor Paul-Marie Duval, who allowed me to range freely over the incomparable collection of offprints on Roman Gaul which forms the Bibliothèque Albert Grenier. I am grateful, too, to the holders of copyright who, in a true scholarly spirit, allowed me to reproduce photographs: Amiens, Museum (5.2); Baldwin, N.Y., Prothman Associates (8.19); Brussels, A.C.L. (7.10); Limoges, Editions modernes Théojac (4.18); Lyon, Musée civique gallo-romain (3.3, 5); Montreal, McGill University Press (8.9); New York, French Government Tourist Office (3.2, 4, 6, 7, 8; 4.6, 14, 15, 17; 8.4, 6, 7, 11); Orléans, Museum (7.4); Paris: *Gallia* (1.9b; 3.9; 6.13); Musée historique de la ville (6.4); Librairie Plon (6.11, 14; 7.6); Rodez, Musée Fenaille (7.7); St.-Bertrand-de-Comminges, M. B. Sapène (4.2a, 3, 4); Semur, Société des sciences historiques (2.7, 8, 10); Sens, Museum (7.3a, b; 4). Others who sold me reproduction rights are listed at the back of the book.

My best thanks again go to my eagle-eyed colleagues, J. P. Heironimus and E. L. Bennett, Jr., for proof-reading.

Paris
August, 1971

Contents

Illustrations

I

Before the Romans

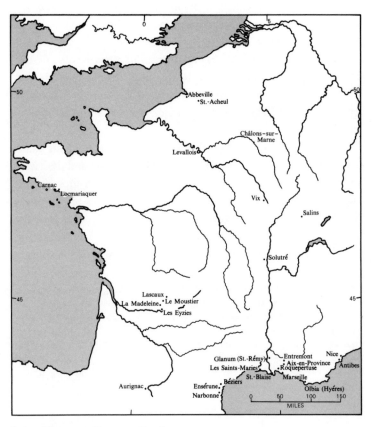

1.1   Map, pre-Roman Gaul

Modern travelers come to France, I suppose, mainly on account of the reputation of her food, her wine, and her women. The Romans, too, relished two out of three of these.*

But the Romans were there not as tourists but to administer an empire and to make money. The province they created has influenced the modern world. In city and villa, it stood off the barbarian, keeping alive both the essence of Romanization (equal justice under law, efficient transport by land and water) and its elegance (Latin language, Roman dress, porticoed buildings, baths, dinner-parties).† The development of these amenities is the subject of this book.

A Greek writing in the reign of Augustus describes the Gauls: brave, strong, individualistic to a fault, excitable, talented, adaptable, living in a land rich and well-watered, a constant temptation to the conqueror. The story goes back into the almost infinite past.

France was inhabited 540,000 years before the Romans came. Because nineteenth-century French archaeologists had the vision and the energy to excavate them first, the habitation sites of these Old Stone Age Frenchmen have given their names to successive phases of Palaeolithic culture. As early as 1838, Jacques Boucher de Perthes was collecting paleolithic artifacts in the gravel-pits of Abbeville (see map, Fig. 1.1‡); other discoveries, as the century

---

*The reputation of French women in antiquity rested mainly on their size, strength, and fecundity. The historian Ammianus Marcellinus, writing late in the fourth Christian century, is particularly entertaining: "A Gallic woman, fighting beside her man, is a match for a whole troop of foreigners. Steely-eyed, and far stronger than her husband, she swells her neck, gnashes her teeth, flexes her huge white biceps, and rains wallops and kicks as though from the twisted cords of a catapult." More a Brünnhilde, one gathers, than a Mimi.

†The list comes from Tacitus, *Agricola* 21.

‡For the names of departments in which sites are located, see Index.

wore on, made it possible to construct an approximate chronology of the paleolithic age as follows:

PALAEOLITHIC CULTURES

Approx. Date B.C.	*Name*	*Type-Site*	*Characteristics*
540,000-325,000	Abbevillian	Abbeville (Somme-et-Marne): see map, Fig. 1.1)	Hand-axes; bones of mammoth, rhinoceros, saber-tooth tiger
325,000-150,000	Acheulian	St.-Acheul (Somme)	Human skulls with brain-pans nearly as large as modern man's
280,000	Levalloisian	Levallois (Haute-de-Seine)	Subdivision of Acheulian; flaked tools from prepared cores
130,000-80,000	Mousterian	Le Moustier (Dordogne)	Cave-dwellings; use of fire
80,000-70,000	Aurignacian	Aurignac (Haute-Garonne)	At type site: 17 human skeletons; bones of horses used for food
70,000-50,000	Solutrean	Solutré (Saône-et-Loire)	Laurel-leaf-shaped stone spearheads
50,000-10,000	Magdalenian	La Madeleine (Dordogne)	Lascaux cave falls late in this period

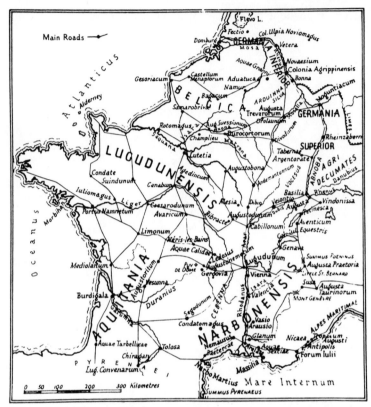

1.1a   Map, Roman Gaul

It is the Magdalenian culture which most excites the imagination of modern man. The Dordogne valley is attractive country,
aptly called the golf course of the gods, a land of steep gorges,
forests of chestnut and poplar, cottages and castles, and, above
all, caves. These were inhabited, 17,000 years ago, by men who
give the lie to the concept "primitive," if by that we mean sham-
bling ape-like men with low foreheads, hairy bodies, a tendency
to club their womenfolk, and no idea of art. For Magdalenian

artists produced, not far from where Caesar was to fight the last campaign of his Gallic Wars, the most famous cave paintings of all time.

A dog named Robot was responsible for the discovery, in the autumn of 1940, of the famous cave paintings of Lascaux, within eight miles of Le Moustier. Out for a run with his master and three other teen-age boys, he literally fell into the cave. The boys, following, burrowed five or six meters straight down, and found by the uncertain light of a flashlight that they were in a high narrow passages, the walls and ceiling of which were covered with paintings of animals in red, yellow, and black (Fig. 1.2). There were some 800 in all, among them wild cattle, bison, shaggy ponies cantering, stags swimming in a lake, wild goats about to lock horns. The cave is 110 yards long. The Rotunda, nearest the entrance, contains the most monumental animal figures in all Palaeolithic art; some, like the colossal bulls with splendidly curving horns visible in the photograph, are more than 17 feet long, over twice the size of the largest figure in Lascaux' only rival, the cave of Altamira in northern Spain.* Though the Carbon-14 date for the main occupation level at Lascaux is *ca.* 15,000 B.C., the paintings went through many phases, and the best of them are dated by experts at about 12,500 B.C. Like those at Altamira, they are probably best interpreted as hunting-magic: the geniuses who painted them had, like good Frenchmen, something to eat in mind. Or if, as some scholars think, the paintings are fertility magic, that too is an appropriate French occupation.

What preserved the paintings was a crystalline deposit. Before they were opened to the public, special precautions were taken: a bronze entrance-door; two antechambers at different levels, to keep the warm air out; constant temperature and humidity control; careful drainage. But the breath, sweat, mud, and dirt introduced by 500 visitors a day caused a deposit of green mold on

Iberian Stones Speak, 3-10.

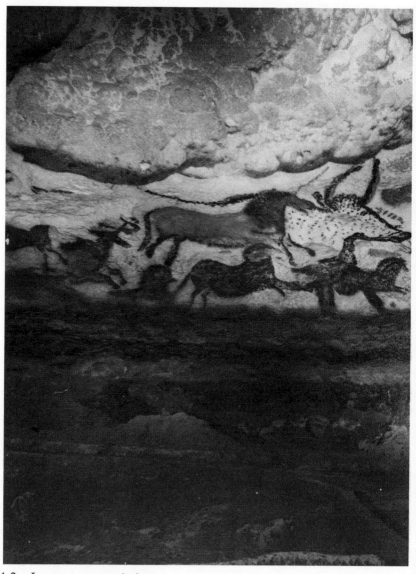

1.2 Lascaux, cave paintings

the paintings. The cave was first closed altogether, then opened
to five visitors a day. A new treatment with antibiotic aerosol
spray and formaldehyde made possible, in August 1969, the
triumphant announcement that the quota was being raised to ten.
The disappointed may see colored films of the wonders in an
anteroom, or visit the scarcely less spectacular paintings in the
caves of La Mouthe or Font-de-Gaume, near neighboring Les
Eyzies. Wonders they are, wherever visited. One of the things
archaeology can do is create perspective and a proper humility.
It sophisticates one's ideas of progress to realize that artists of
genius were painting in France over 14,000 years before Picasso.

Among the most remarkable pre-Roman monuments of France
must be included the Bronze Age alignments of *menhirs*—
literally "long stones"—at Carnac (Morbihan) in Brittany, near
where Julius Caesar over 1400 years later was to defeat the Veneti
at sea. Carnac is in the center of a district containing the world's
most remarkable megaliths. There are over 3,000 in a stretch of
less than two and a half miles (Fig. 1.3). One group of 1099 ex-
tends in eleven rows, with stones ranging from thirteen feet in
height down to three. One menhir now lying broken into four
pieces, at Locmariaquer, is sixty-seven feet long, and weighs
342 tons. The alignments are oriented to sunrise at the equinox
or solstices, and must, like Stonehenge across the Channel, have
had a religious and/or funerary significance. They often point to
a burial-mound or barrow, containing bell-beakers, gold plaques
(more Bronze Age gold has been found in Brittany than anywhere else in France), arrowheads, pendants, incised pottery, and
very fine parade axes in dolerite or jadeite. They are dated by the
presence in them of faïence (blue glass paste), segmented beads
which were imported from Egypt, where they occur in dated con-
texts of about 1400 B.C. These contacts with the outside world
are typical of the megalith builders: the occurrence of these huge
monuments along the Atlantic littoral of Europe suggests the

1.3   Carnac, megaliths

spread of religious ideas by missionaries who were also traders. Whatever their origin, they have been rightly called the greatest and most imaginative monuments of any people dependent upon a primitive rural economy.

The megalith builders may have been Iberians, but the ultimate source of their inspiration was Greek. Greeks came early to the south of France: Rhodian pottery of the seventh century B.C. has been found in the excavations of St.-Blaise. The site is noteworthy chiefly for its walls (Fig. 1.4), a piece of Greek military architecture unique in Gaul. Built of carefully squared blocks fitted together without mortar, they rise from twenty feet in height to thirty at the towers, and are seven to twelve feet thick. Their

1.4   St.-Blaise, Greek walls

footings go down to bedrock. Within the walls there is evidence
of a gridded street-plan, with narrow sidewalks. The pottery, the
archaeologist's best clue to dates, shows a blank in the fifth century B.C., when the Greeks were busy with wars at home, and the
Carthaginians controlled the western Mediterranean. The pottery
before the blank period comes from Rhodes, Ionia, Athens,
Corinth, and Etruria; afterwards, it comes chiefly from south Italy
and Spain, and there are coins from nearby Marseille. Warehouses contain amphoras (wine and oil jars) with South Italian
stamps; there are shops where lead, bronze, and iron were
worked. On the acropolis, piers with holes for the insertion of
severed heads were found. These show that this originally Greek
foundation became Gallic in culture, for severed heads were a
Gallic, not a Greek fixation. An ancient Greek historian tells us
that the Gauls used to cut off their enemies' heads and sling them
at their saddlebows, singing their victory song the while. They

would nail the heads to the walls of their living-rooms, or embalm
them in cedar oil and keep them in chests, and could not be in-
duced to sell them for their weight in gold. Mute evidence of
St.-Blaise's final fate is found in a trench containing thirty-nine
large stone catapult-balls, ranging in weight from eight to forty
pounds. These were fired by Romans when Julius Caesar was
besieging Marseille and its environs in 49 B.C.

Marseille, the oldest and, according to some, the wickedest city
in France, was founded by Asiatic Greeks from Phocaea in about
600 B.C. The attraction was its fine harbor, the Vieux Port (Fig.
1.5) beside which a fine small museum houses the antiquities

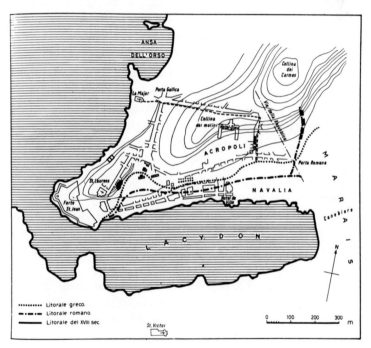

1.5   Marseille, plan

found nearby. They span the whole ancient history of the place: stoppered jars which once contained oil, wine, fish sauce (a much-esteemed delicacy), olives, perfume, or pitch for caulking ships; wooden caulking tools, anchors of lead and stone, lead and copper ingots probably used for ballast, sounding leads, net-weights; a rope-walk, a Hellenistic haulway, the piles of the Roman port, the keel of a ship found in 1864. The general impression is nautical and salty: Marseille has always been a sailors' town, with its labyrinth of steep, dark streets around the harbor. It made its money from seaborne commerce, the transit trade, and commissions. As early as 535 B.C. it was rich enough to dedicate a treasury at the Greek international shrine of Apollo at Delphi. At the height of its prosperity, in the fourth and third centuries B.C., its economic dominance spread along the coast in both directions. Riviera resorts like Nice and Antibes (Antipolis, the city across the bay from Nice) owe their foundation to Marseille: Nice (Nicaea, Victory City) was named for a Massiliote victory over the Etruscans. A Massiliote trading-station, Olbia, on the sea near Hyères, was excavated in the early 'fifties. In the third or second century B.C. it had a wall measuring 460 by 400 feet, built of square blocks set without mortar, like St.-Blaise. Within the wall were a grid of streets, warehouses, and a portico, but the pottery was Roman, not Greek, testifying to the way in which Marseille was commercially engulfed by her Roman alliance.

Marseille traded with Spain, Italy, Sicily, Sardinia, Corsica, and Carthage, and hoards of coins show the part she played in the economic development of the Rhône valley. Marseille was the home port of the most famous explorer of antiquity, Pytheas, an ancient Columbus who, between 310 and 306 B.C., coasted along Africa as far as Senegal, saw the Sargasso Sea, and sailed through the fogs of the north Atlantic and around Scotland, where he saw icebergs, whales, and the midnight sun.

However free and easy the sailors may have been, the Marseille Establishment was aristocratic and conservative. Laws limited expenditure on works of art, and so artistic finds are sparse. Massiliote conservatism was in sympathy with Rome's. Marseille helped the Romans against Carthage, so that when the Carthaginian Hannibal set out from Spain to invade Italy in 218 B.C., he crossed the Rhône far upriver, for fear of Marseille. But these services got small rewards: when Rome took over the Carthaginian sphere of influence in Spain, Marseille lost her commercial predominance, and the area of Massiliote sway became, in 118 B.C., Rome's first Gallic province, Narbonensis, *the* province *par excellence;* hence its modern name, Provence. Marseille's famed fish soup, bouillabaisse, made it a favorite place of exile for gourmet Romans at odds with the ruling powers. Mark Antony's son Lucius was exiled thither "for studies" at the university, and stayed so long (twenty-seven years) that he became the senior student. The father-in-law of the Roman historian Tacitus, Agricola, was born in nearby Fréjus, and was sent to Marseille to study; there he could acquire Greek manners cheap. He grew up to make a name for himself as a conquering general in Britain.

Marseille's conservatism led her to support the Roman general Pompey against Caesar in their struggle for power. As a consequence the city was besieged, under Caesar's personal command; he describes his elaborate siegeworks in his *Commentaries on the Civil War.* Marseille fell in 49 B.C., after holding out desperately for six months, losing its prosperity but not its autonomy.

A temple of Artemis has been found under the old cathedral; a stretch of the Hellenistic wall and the theater were excavated in 1967. Under Nero a Massiliote physician, Crinas, a descendant of Pytheas the navigator, subsidized the building of walls, parts of which were unearthed near the harbor in the nineteenth and twentieth centuries. In the Christian tradition, a local legend has it that Lazarus, after Christ raised him from the dead, became Marseille's first bishop! And at Les-Saintes-Maries-de-la-Mer, forty-five miles to the west, Mary the sister of the Virgin, Salome the mother of James and John, and their black servant Sara are supposed to have been cast up in a ship without sails or oars; the fortified church which marks the spot is an object of pilgrimage to this day.

Thus the triple heritage of Marseille and its environs, from Greece, Rome, and Christianity, gives it a special claim to our attention.

Marseille may have been the port of transshipment for the most impressive piece of Greek metalwork ever found in France, or anywhere else for that matter, the bronze *crater* (punchbowl) of Vix (Fig. 1.6). It was found in January 1953, the most striking of fifty-three objects in the wood-lined chamber of a *tumulus* (burial mound) 138 feet across, which was being excavated near Châtillon-sur-Seine. It stands over 5 feet tall, and weighs 436 pounds. Snake-haired Gorgons decorate the handles; between the handles runs a frieze of chariots, charioteers, and warriors wearing the armor fashionable in the Ripe Archaic period, the late sixth century B.C. The body of the vase was made in one piece, without soldering, beaten when cold, and polished. Each of the men and horses in the frieze differs slightly from every other, so that it is clear this is the loving hand-work of a craftsman of genius, and not made from molds. The bowl has a cover, weighing 30 pounds; in its center the statuette of a goddess, six inches high, wearing a belted, pleated robe and a Mona Lisa smile.

This masterpiece and the noteworthy accompanying treasures were intended to comfort the afterlife of a princess whose skeleton, on a bier, was found in the burial chamber. She was wearing her jewels: bracelets of bronze, amber, coral, and gold; an amber necklace; and a diadem of gold filigree. Among the treasures buried with her were a plain silver bowl, an Attic black-figure cup portraying warriors and Amazons, an Etruscan bronze pitcher, three bronze basins with lotus-and-palmette handles, and

1.6   Vix, bronze mixing bowl

the princess's funeral car, in which she lay on her bier, covered
with a pall in red and blue. The princess's burial place lies directly
on the route by which tin, so essential for the making of bronze,

was imported from Cornwall to Mediterranean lands; her great wealth was no doubt derived from levying tolls upon the tin-traders.

Pre-Roman Gaul had its native towns, called *oppida*, of which the model is Ensérune, between Béziers and Narbonne. It lies on a triangular thirty-seven-acre plateau, 400 feet above the fertile coastal plain, with a view of a vast horizon of sea and mountain. Scientific excavation, with careful attention to levels and datable pottery, showed that it was first settled about 550 B.C. Its dwellings were huts some twelve feet across, made of wicker-work plastered with mud, in the technique called wattle-and-daub, with pits for food storage in the floors. There was house-hold debris in the pits: sheep and pig bones, shellfish, and loom-weights, proving that the women knew how to weave. It was a backward commmunity, a survival from the Stone Age; some of the tools were still made of stone, and the pottery was hand-made, not wheel-turned.

In the next phase, dated by pottery at the end of the fifth century B.C., the villagers were living in rough stone houses, on ter-races linked by stairs. Their living-rooms had painted stucco walls, and they collected water in cisterns lined with waterproof cement. The settlement was surrounded with a circuit wall, built of large irregular stones in the technique called Cyclopean; on the north slope, houses (Fig. 1.7), preserved to a height of over six feet, abut the wall.

The third phase, which begins about 225 B.C., shows Roman influence in the building techniques and the pottery, but the lan-guage was Iberian and not Latin, as is proved by graffiti on some of the pots. From about 400 to 250 B.C., the west end of the pla-teau was used as a burial ground: The graves—over 250 of them —yielded weapons (deliberately bent), shields, sword-chains, belt buckles, *fibulae* (safety-pins), bracelets, rings, earrings, beads

1.7   Ensérune, Gallic oppidum north slope houses

of blue glass paste; the ashes of the cremated dead were collected in valuable Italian or Greek vases, not local ware.

The excavation showed that this native Gallic village was open to four influences—Greek, Celtic, Iberian, and Roman. The Greek influence was economic, not political. It has a symbol in mythology: the legend of Heracles' cattle-rustling travels between Spain and Italy. The Greek influence is clearest in the pottery. At first it comes from Ionia (Asia Minor) then, from about 525 to 490 B.C., from Athens—the characteristic black-figure ware. Then for two generations Athenian pottery ceases: this represents the years (490–425) when the Carthaginians cut off Athenian trade. For the next century, the pottery is Attic again. About 330, Ensérune began to import from south Italy (also Greek at this time) and finally, in the first century B.C., Campanian ware, which is Roman, begins. Coins, too, show Greek economic penetration. They are mostly from Marseille till the beginning of the second century B.C., when local mints began to operate in Béziers (using a Greek alphabet) and Narbonne (using Iberian). Gauls, including no doubt some from Ensérune, served as mercenaries in Greek armies, but they only imitated Greek culture; they were not penetrated by it.

The Celtic influence is visible in the metalwork: the heavy bronze neck-rings called torques, for men, rings and bracelets, tool handles, coins, all with a decoration at once unrestrained and abstract, a far cry from Greek ideals of order and symmetry. There is no question of political domination: it was against the Celts that the villagers of Ensérune built their circuit wall.

Iberian influence is more profound. The graffiti leave no doubt that Iberian was the local language, and Catalonian sites like Ullastret* show a way of life so similar to that of Ensérune that we must conclude that before the Romans there was but one culture on either side of the Pyrenees.

Roman influence becomes conspicuous after the Romans founded their colony at Narbo Martius, (the later Narbonne), less than six miles away, in 118 B.C. There was no need for the Romans to take over Ensérune. A careful watch from Narbonne was enough. The natives imitated Roman building techniques: waterproof cement, stone paving, tiled roofs, stucco. They did not adopt Roman comforts; their houses were unheated. Roman coins circulated, Roman pottery came into use, but not the Latin language. In sum, what the excavations at Ensérune have unearthed is six centuries of the history of a native people rooted in prehistory, but independent, though open to cultural influences from abroad, as the French have been ever since.

When Caesar wrote "All Gaul is divided into three parts,"

*Iberian Stones Speak, 61-72.

(Belgians, Aquitanians, and Celts or Gauls) his intelligence service could tell him very little about the three peoples he was to conquer. Modern archaeology can tell us more, especially about the Celts in what are now the departments of Marne and Jura, in central and east central France, before the Romans came.

The Celts had a common language, which survives in Breton, Cornish, Welsh and Gaelic, and a common artistic tradition, whose decoration shows an exuberant taste for swinging, swelling curves, very far indeed from Graeco-Roman notions of classical restraint. Equipped with iron weapons and chariots, the Celts, led by warrior aristocracy, swept into France from central Europe, perhaps about 750 B.C. This is the Hallstatt phase of their culture, named from a site near Salzburg in Austria where numerous burials containing Celtic artifacts were found. (As usual with pre-literate people, we learn about Celts living from Celts dead.)

A typical Hallstatt site, of 700–500 B.C., is Salins, nowadays a spa, twenty-five miles west of the Swiss border on the main road from Lausanne to Paris. In Celtic times it was a fortified place, an *oppidum,* Camp de Château, two miles from the modern town. It resembles Ensérune. Near it was a cemetery, where 30,000 graves yielded weapons, bronze cauldrons, local pottery of fine gray ware, with stripes incised with a comb, and, most precious to the archaeologist, imported Greek vases, black- and red-figured ware which can be closely dated, to the late sixth and early fifth centuries B.C.

The best-known Celtic oppida were excavated for three reasons: They survived into Caesar's time; they come in to his story of his Gallic campaigns; and their nineteenth-century excavators were more interested in their Roman conquerors than in their conquered ancestors. Three of these sites, Bibracte, (Mt. Beuvray, near Autun, Saône-et-Loire); Gergovia (Puy-de-Dôme); and Alesia (Alise-Ste.-Reine, Côte-d'Or), will be discussed, in their later phases, in the next chapter.

In this chapter, our interest is in the archaeological evidence for the phase of the Celtic Iron Age which followed the Hallstatt period. It is called La Tène, after a site on Lake Neuchâtel in Switzerland, and extended from about 450 B.C. to the beginning of the Christian era. We know most about it from thousands of burials—evidence for a dense population—in the Champagne area of the Marne valley, centering around Châlons-sur-Marne. The richest burials are those of Celtic warrior-chiefs, who liked to take with them to the after-life the things that had given them most pleasure and profit in this one: their chariots were dismantled, the wheels placed upright in slots dug at both sides of the corpse, the chariot-pole and harness at the owner's feet, the wicker-panelled sides adjacent. The chiefs took with them, too, their swords and daggers; their swastika-engraved, pointed, coral-knobbed helmets; armlets, bracelets, and rings of bronze or sometimes gold; Greek bronze pitchers, and choice Greek red-figured vases, perhaps paid for by exporting the chariots and wagons for which Celtic Gaul was famous in the Greek and Roman worlds. Their favorite food was also buried with them: one grave contained the skeleton of a whole boar, another—a delightfully French touch—frogs' legs! The modern traveler can see the contents of some of these graves on display in the local museum, or, more conveniently, in the French National Museum at St.-Germain-en-Laye, only a dozen miles west of Paris.

For centuries, the warriors who once drove these chariots and brandished these swords struck fear into Roman hearts. In 390 B.C. they held the city of Rome itself to ransom; in 279 they attacked Apollo's oracle at Delphi, and streamed on into central Asia Minor; St. Paul addressed their descendants as Galatians. In the Gallic homeland, they were a constant threat to the Greeks and Romans settled in Provence, and if only they had resisted their fatal tendency to inter-tribal squabbles, they could have united to hold off Caesar, in which case this book would be telling a very different story.

Ensérune, Salins, and the Marne cemeteries offer archaeological proof that Gaul was indigenous before it was Roman; Marseille shows it was also Greek. Our next site, Glanum, provides architectural evidence for all three cultures. Glanum, just south of St.-Rémy, and fifteen miles northeast of Arles, lies in country that entranced Van Gogh, in a narrow valley overlooked by the rocky, pine-clad slopes of the Alpilles (Fig. 1.8). Here, in the sixth and fifth centuries B.C., a native shrine arose by the cave of a divinity believed to have healing powers. By the third century, Greeks

1.8   Glanum, general view

had settled beside the natives. The best evidence of this phase, called Glanum I, is the bouleuterion, or council chamber (plan, Fig. 1.9, XXII), originally a 40 by 25-foot rectangular building with seats rising in steps around the interior wall. There is a very similar building in Hellenistic Priene, in Asia Minor.* The

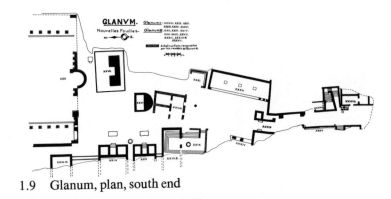

1.9   Glanum, plan, south end

double treasury opposite the bouleuterion is also Hellenistic, and so is the Doric portico (XXXII): the evidence is Massiliote coins, which were fused in a fire which destroyed the building at the end of the second century B.C. The portico may have been a dormitory for pilgrims who came to be cured at the healing spring.

Hellenistic Greek buildings are rare in Gaul, so that Glanum is a site of great archaeological interest. And not only for its public buildings. The private houses, too, are Hellenistic in their lowest levels. The house plans with their peristyles (porticoed gardens), clearly visible in the air view (Fig. 1.10), find their closest parallel on the Aegean island of Delos. The house in the right center of the photograph, with its twelve columns around a

*Greek Stones Speak, 311; paperback, 289.

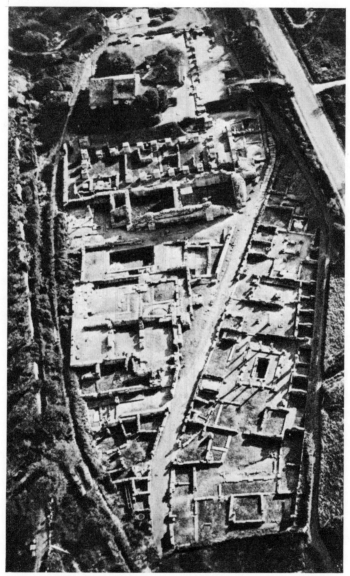

1.10   Glanum: air view

pool, originally had two stories, and one of the stair-treads was repaired in antiquity with an inscription in re-use. There are pebble-mosaic paving, walls painted with gay panels in primary colors, a latrine flushed with running water from the pool, and a stable-annex, identified by the marks of the hubs of the high-wheeled wagons that scraped the side of the stable door. Among the finds in this house (VI on the plan, Fig. 1.11, which corresponds to the airview, Fig. 1.10) were a statuette of a crouching black and a rock crystal ring engraved in intaglio. The pottery shows that the house lasted down into Roman times.

In the last decade of the second century B.C., the Rhône valley was overrun by Germanic invaders, the Cimbri, who came from Jutland. It was probably they who destroyed Hellenistic Glanum. After the Roman general Marius defeated them in 101, the little city revived: the archaeologists call it Glanum II. Its remains, too, are of great interest, for very little such evidence of Roman occupation before Caesar survives in Gaul. For example, the baths visible to the left of the main street in Fig. 1.10 are Roman, dated about 80 B.C. because of their resemblance to the Forum baths of Pompeii, which are of that date. The Glanum baths had gaily-painted walls and glass windows. They lasted down into the Empire: to this phase belong the *palaestra* (exercise ground) and the

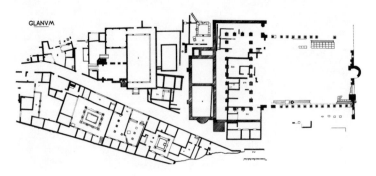

1.11   Glanum, plan, north end

pool visible above it in Fig. 1.10, in which north is at the bottom. The apsidal building to the south, shown in detail in Fig. 1.8, is also Roman. It was probably the basilica, used as a combination law-court and covered market, and possibly built by Augustus' lieutenant Agrippa about 20 B.C. It replaced a house in which a surviving graffito of the "Kilroy was here" variety bears a date corresponding to March 28, 32 B.C. South of it the air photograph shows the twenty-four piers of a porticoed building which overlooked the Forum, further excavated since the air photograph was taken. This is a porticoed court paved with flagstones and measuring 135 by 100 feet. It was faced with limestone, and had statues of satyrs in the niches at its south end. The large apse may have held a statue of Augustus, for the excavators assign this building, too, to his faithful lieutenant. South of the apse is a triumphal monument (Fig. 1.9, XXVII), dated A.D. 75-100, perhaps commemorating the German campaigns of the Emperor Domitian.

Just to the south of this monument is the area which had contained the public and religious monuments of Glanum I: bouleuterion, treasury, and portico. The Romans continued to use the area for the same purposes. Between 9 and 7 B.C. twin temples to Augustus' grandsons, Gaius and Lucius (Fig. 1.9, XXIV-XXV) were built in a U-shaped portico southwest of the Forum. In the well between the temples were found the heads of statues of Augustus' sister Octavia and his daughter Julia, who was married to Agrippa. Southeast of the Forum a small theater was built about the same time, probably for religious pageants connected with the healing cult. The building numbered XXXVI is identified by an inscription as a shrine to Valetudo (Health), dedicated by Agrippa; the adjoining building (XXXVII) was a shrine of Hercules, as a statue and altars prove. Across the Via Sacra to the west was found an inscription, GLAN, presumably the healing divinity for whom Glanum was named.

Roman Glanum's two most impressive surviving monuments,

called locally *Les Antiques*, remain to be described. They lie to
the north of the monuments previously mentioned, at the entrance
to the ancient town. The earlier of the two is the Mausoleum of
the Julii (Fig. 1.12). Statues of the C. Julius who commissioned
the monument, and of his wife, stand under the conical roof at
the top. They were probably rich Gauls, given citizenship by
Julius Caesar, but in the reliefs they selected to decorate the base
of their monument they advertise their acquaintance with Greek

1.12   St.-Rémy, mausoleum of Julii

culture, for the motifs are all mythological: Theseus fighting the Amazons, the battle between the Lapiths and the Centaurs, the Calydonian boar hunt, the deaths of Adonis and the children of Niobe, and the heroic deeds of Achilles' friend Patroclus. But all these mythological figures are in modern dress: the warriors wear the armor that was in fashion in 40 B.C.

Beside the mausoleum stands a monumental arch (Fig. 1.13), generally held to be Agrippa's work, like the basilica. The reliefs

1.13   St.-Rémy, arch

on its face show Gallic captives chained to trophies; on the west
side, a Roman grants a captured Gaul his liberty; on the ends are
implements used in sacrifices: knives, libation bowls, a *thyrsos*
(a pine cone on a pole, carried by worshippers of the wine-god
Bacchus), as well as musical instruments, including a double flute,
cymbals, and the curved trumpet called a *lituus*. Framing the
archway is a frieze of oak leaves, acorns, grapevines, grapes, ivy,
pine cones, pomegranates, and sprays of olive: much the same
flora occur on Augustus' Altar of Peace in Rome, dedicated in
13 B.C. The message the arch is meant to convey is of Rome's
mission, stated by Vergil in the *Aeneid* (19 B.C.) "To spare the
meek, and battle down the proud."

Between St.-Blaise and Aix, on the rocky spur of Roquepertuse, lies a Gallic sanctuary whose life extended from the fifth to
the second century B.C. The approach is by a narrow natural
bridge, and the sanctuary stands on a 95 by 213-foot plateau.
The one-room houses were not intended to be permanent, as the
sanctuary was in use only for a seasonal festival. The excavators
found sculptures of severed heads, and pillars with put-holes for
skulls. The most important find, known since 1873, and now in
the Musée Borély in nearby Marseille, gives proof of the independence of native art forms. It is the figure of a heroized chief
(Fig. 1.14), seated cross-legged, like a tailor or a Buddha, in what
we shall see was a typically Gallic pose. He was carved by a
local sculptor, remotely but not fundamentally influenced by
Greek conventions. The figure wears a type of chasuble incised
with lozenges picked out in red, with squares, and with swas-
tikas; it is probably intended to represent leather. This hieratic,
forceful, and noble figure is dated on stylistic grounds in the late
third or early second century B.C.

Of all Gallic sculpture the most characteristic is the severed
head, a substitute for the real thing which came into use in the sec-

1.14   Marseille, statue of heroized chief, from Roquepertuse

ond century B.C. The one illustrated (Fig. 1.15) is in the historical
museum of the French nation, set up in the château of St.-Ger-
main-en-Laye, near Paris. The head comes from Entremont, the

Gallic oppidum which preceded the Roman foundation of Aquae
Sextiae (Aix-en-Provence), and lies just under two miles northwest of that city. Entremont was the capital of the Gallo-Ligurian
tribe of the Saluvii, and though its area is less than nine acres, it
has a well-built circuit wall, elegant houses in the upper city, and,
in the lower, an artisans' quarter which yielded an olive press and
evidence of Gallic metalwork, such as anvils, tongs, hammers,
and a 100-kilo block of lead. Our sculpture, as well as skulls with

1.15   Entremont, severed head

nail holes driven through them, came from the town's sanctuary. Ironically, the civilized instinct which prompted the transition from the real severed head to its sculptured replica had a softening effect: in 123 B.C. the Romans successfully besieged the place. The evidence is the catapult balls, weighing eight to eighteen pounds, which prove that the fall of Entremont was not due to barbarians. Only Romans were civilized enough to use siege-engines. And the Romans would naturally wreak vengeance on an enemy who not many years before had been so keen on decapitation. So the place was sacked, and the Romans founded Aquae Sextiae in the plain below. Twenty years later, on a battlefield overlooked by Cézanne's favorite mountain, Ste.-Victoire, Gaius Marius defeated the Teutons. The carnage was so frightful that for years afterwards the fields there yielded remarkable crops, fertilized by the blood of the fallen, and farmers fenced their fields with the bones of the victims. At the time of the victory, Narbonese Gaul had been a Roman province for eighteen years. Two years after the victory, a child was born who was to make the whole of Gaul essentially Roman forever. His name was Julius Caesar.

II

Caesar Slept Here

2.1 Map: Caesar's campaigns in Gaul

33

"You cannot visit a single city of France," wrote Voltaire, "without hearing some good people boast of having had Caesar in their midst. Each province competes with its neighbor for the honor of having been the first to which Caesar gave a flogging. We quarrel over which route he used to come and slit our throats, make love to our wives and daughters, impose laws on us by interpreter, and steal our tiny savings. An Italian archaeologist, on a visit to Vannes in Brittany a few years ago, was astonished to hear the local savants brag of Caesar's stay in their city. 'You have, no doubt,' he inquired, 'some memorial of this great man?' 'Yes,' replied their spokesman, 'we can show you the spot where this paragon had our entire provincial senate hanged.' "

Voltaire is being unfair, as usual. If atrocities were all that Roman imperialism meant to Gaul, this book would not be worth writing except to record horrible examples. Undeniable instances of Roman murder, rape, tyranny, and pillage are on the record, but what the Romans won in the horror of war they caused to prosper by the arts of peace, as we shall see. It is sheer, perverse romanticism to find, in the teeth of the evidence, nothing but one long series of calculated brutalities in the archaeological and historical record of Roman Gaul. Stephen Vincent Benét, addressing an imaginary Roman about his empire, has put the case more justly than Voltaire: "You brought nothing but an arch, a road, an army, and a law. Yet a man might walk from the east to the west of it; yes, and speak the same tongue all the way. I do not admire you, but you were a great people."

A word must be said—though the evidence is mostly not archaeological—about Roman Provence from its founding to Caesar's arrival. Of the capital, Narbo Martius (Narbonne, see map, Fig. 2.1), the surviving remains—a huge Capitolium, the Forum, a warehouse, an amphitheater—are later than our period, but they testify to the material prosperity which Rome brought to Gaul. The colony's founder, Cn. Domitius Ahenobarbus, was the grandfather of one of Caesar's most inveterate enemies, and, incidentally, the remote ancestor of the Emperor Nero. Domitius sited his colony within three miles of the Mediterranean, and built the strategically important Via Domitia, connecting Italy with Spain; it formed the main street of the colony. Narbo was Rome's second overseas colony (the first was at Carthage), and its epithet "Martius," dedicating it to the god of war, is significant of the military motivation for its planting. Caesar himself, in 46 B.C., settled the veterans of his favorite Tenth Legion, the *Decumani,* there; after which it became the *Colonia Iulia Paterna Decumanorum.* Cicero speaks of it as a "watchtower and bulwark of the Roman people."

Narbo became the seat of the Roman governors of the Provincia Narbonensis. The most notorious of these, M. Fonteius (in office 76-74 B.C.), owes his dubious fame to a speech of Cicero's in his defense (69 B.C.) on a charge of malfeasance in office. The plaintiffs were certain provincials, whom Cicero describes, rather unfairly, as clad in plaid and breeches—trousers, to a Roman, always symbolized barbarism. Their word, he said, was not to be trusted, they were addicted to human sacrifice, and they were Rome's sworn enemies, having once, in 390 B.C., besieged Rome's sacred Capitolium itself. This is irrelevant advocacy, but it suggests the image of the Gauls to which Caesar might appeal at need, to justify his career of conquest. The Roman colonists settled at Narbonne, Cicero says, were for Fonteius, as were Rome's allies and friends like the Massiliotes, and the Roman businessmen in Provence. And well they might be: "No Gaul," Cicero says, "does a stroke of business without a Roman citizen; not a coin changes hands without appearing on the books of a Roman banker." The plaintiffs, understandably, thought of themselves as exploited provincials: Fonteius had drafted cavalry from them, quartered soldiers on them, requisitioned grain, made them work on road repair, and taxed their wine. These were the sort of practices used by the American colonists to justify their revolution in 1776; in 69 B.C. they were the normal demands made

upon a subject people. But the Gauls complained that Fonteius
had gone further. He was getting kickbacks from the tax-collec-
tors; exempting individuals, for a fee, from the *corvée* and their
taxes; turning a blind eye to fraudulent contractors; and illegally
confiscating property. Nevertheless, the defendant was acquitted.
Two years later he bought an expensive house in Naples. The
Gauls had their revenge in the end: excesses of this kind contributed to the downfall of the Roman Republic, and Augustus
and his successors reformed the provincial administration. It was
Tiberius, not himself the best of Emperors, who remarked of tax
policy, "We should shear our sheep, not skin them."

Not all members of the Roman ruling class in Gaul behaved
as badly as Fonteius. Caesar's great rival, Pompey the Great, was
a benign patron. He settled his defeated foes, the veterans of
Sertorius' uprising in Spain*, in a pleasant colony in the foothills
of the Pyrenees, Lugdunum Convenarum, nowadays St. Bertrand-
de-Comminges. None of its remains is as old as its founding, but
we shall see in a later chapter how it prospered.

The inhabitants of what the Romans called "Hairy Gaul"
(Gallia Comata) were themselves responsible for calling the
Romans in, to save them from invasion or from inter-tribal fac-
tion. In 61 B.C. the Aedui sent a member of their ruling class, the
Druid Diviciacus, to Rome to ask the Senate for aid against an
invading German tribe, the Suebi, under the arrogant Ariovistus.
The Senate did not act then. But three years later, an aggressive,
ambitious proconsul, Julius Caesar, was only too glad of any excuse to intervene in Gaul, and win a war to make his prestige
rival Pompey's. He found a pretext ready to hand. The Helvetii,
who lived north of Lake Geneva, burned their villages and their
surplus grain, and began a mass migration—of 368,000 people,
Caesar says—across Gaul to a new home on the Atlantic coast.
Caesar, pretending that their trek menaced Rome's interests in
Provence, hurried to Geneva to stop them.

ISS, 117-120.

What we know archaeologically about his preventive measures we owe to the vanity of the French emperor Napoleon III, who, fancying himself the modern reincarnation of his hero, surrounded himself with archaeologists and other savants, and published, five years before his defeat in the Franco-Prussian War, the two volumes of his *Histoire de Jules César*, with its beautifully engraved and colored maps which have been standard ever since. Napoleon's chief archaeological aide, the Alsatian Col. Stoffel, carefully surveyed the route of the Helvetian exodus along the Rhône from Lake Geneva, where Caesar had kept them under observation to prevent them from turning toward Provence. Stoffel found three miles of Roman trenches, and four castella, sited to afford the maximum view, all within five hours' march of Geneva. Caesar could make do with a minimum number of forts, because this stretch of the Rhône mostly has steep banks, and was thus naturally inaccesible to the enemy. Stoffel calculated that Caesar needed only 10,000 men to turn back the unwieldy mass of 368,000, encumbered as they must have been. They would have needed 12,420 tons of grain, 8,500 wagons, and 24,000 draft animals; it took them twenty days to cover the sixty miles from Geneva to the Saône. They made their last stand at Toulon-sur-Arroux, sixteen miles south of the important Gallic stronghold of Bibracte, now called Mt. Beuvray (Côte-d'Or). There were only 130,000 survivors, whom Caesar made return to their scorched earth.

To us, Caesar's victory over the wretched Helvetians may appear to be on a level with shooting fish in a barrel, but it made the impression he desired in Rome. And hard on its heels came another request from the Aeduans for help against the Germans: success in this venture would build the proconsul's prestige still higher. The request came at a meeting of a council of the Gauls at their bleak, windy oppidum of Bibracte, 2,567 feet above the sea. Nowadays there is a motor road to the top, but the Gauls negotiated the icy hill on foot. The *crampons* they used for climbing were found on the site. The place has been excavated, and is of particular interest as being almost completely Gallic. Late in the century (perhaps in 12, perhaps in 7 B.C.), the Romans moved the entire population to their new city, Augustodunum (Autun), fifteen miles east, in the plain. The excavators at Mt. Beuvray found a house full of skeletons, as though the townsfolk wanted to gather their dead in a safe place before leaving their oppidum forever. It was a sizeable town; the perimeter of the wall is three miles, enclosing 333 acres. Over 1,000 Gallic coins were found, including a mint-fresh one of Dumnorix, the Aeduan leader who was Caesar's mortal enemy to the end. Prosperity came from metal- and enamelwork, for which the Gauls were famous. Smithies and enamelworkers' shops were found, together with samples of their craftsmanship, now on display in the Musée Rollin in Autun. The archaeologists found the chief's house, larger and better-built than the rest, the rooms grouped round an atrium, Roman-fashion. They noted that the women's and children's rooms faced north, to toughen their occupants at an altitude where it is winter for six months of the year.

Even after the population was displaced, a fair continued to be held at the old site, in honor of the goddess Bibracte: the excavators found the horse-corrals, and the tradesmen's booths. Bibracte is full of history. There, in 52 B.C., the Gauls of the resistance elected Vercingetorix their leader, clashing their spears on their shields in acclamation. Mark Antony, Caesar's lieutenant, had a camp here. It measured 300 by 360 feet (two and a half acres), which meant that it could house 500 men, since Romans could crowd 220 men into an acre.

Caesar beat the German Ariovistus near Mulhouse, in Alsace, the area of the Belfort Gap, destined to be the scene of bloody fighting in the Franco-Prussian War and again in World War II. The few Germans who escaped did so by swimming the Rhine. Caesar had fought two campaigns in a single summer. His communiqué to the Senate in Rome (*Gallic War*, Book I) had started by justifying an offensive, but it ended by making peace seem illogical. Seven communiqués later, all Gaul was to be at his feet, and also, in due course, the Senate.

The following year (57 B.C.) Caesar used the excuse that the Belgians were "conspiring" to justify a campaign in the northeast. This hapless area has been so scarred by centuries of warfare, including trenches in World War I and aerial bombardment in World War II, that ancient traces of man's inhumanity to man are hard to make out, but two camps have been identified. One is a bridgehead camp of 100 acres, surrounded by a moat twenty feet wide and ten feet deep at Mauchamp, near Berry-au-Bac. Five gates were found, all ingeniously contrived to force anyone entering to make a quarter-turn, exposing his shieldless side to the defenders.

The other camp is at Nointel, near Clermont: Caesar used it in the last campaign of the war in 51 B.C. Here an irregular enclosure of 250 acres contains three camps, two of 55 acres each, for the legions, and one of 4 acres, for Caesar's bodyguard. There were also two outlying camps for loyal native troops. To the west was an earthwork with a wickerwork palisade, protected by eleven half-acre *castella* for hundred-man detachments (centuries). Two log and brushwood causeways, each 2,000 feet long, enabled the legions to cross the marsh which lay between them and the enemy. Caesar's army engineers first staked down bundles of brushwood. Over these they laid oak and alder logs, first crosswise, then lengthwise; over the logs is wickerwork, sprinkled with sand. The causeways widen from 12 feet to 60 at the end toward the enemy, to enable troops to form company front for the assault.

At the news of the success of Caesar's campaign of 57, the Senate in Rome declared an unprecedented fifteen-day holiday. The next year Caesar's legions took to the sea, and defeated the Veneti of Brittany in a naval battle in Quiberon Bay. Recent surveys have discovered a number of earthworks built by the Veneti and their allies against the Romans. One at Huelgoat covers seventy-five acres; another at Le Châtellier, of forty-two acres, had double defensive walls twelve feet high, reinforced with wooden beams. The cliff castle at Kercaradec covered five and a half acres and had multiple ramparts. All these defenses proved vain, and the surviving Veneti fled across the Channel to Britain.

Caesar's abortive attempts in 55/4 B.C. to invade Britain and Germany are not our concern. He campaigned again in the northeast in 53 and thought Gaul was pacified, but he reckoned without the strength of the Gallic resistance movement, which massacred Roman businessmen at Cenabum (Orléans), and, under the heroic leadership of Vercingetorix (Fig. 2.2), found unity and, for a time, success. Modern Frenchmen, proud of their Resistance in World War II, have made Vercingetorix a symbol. He was to the French what Viriathus was to the Portuguese, and Arminius to the Germans.* Camille Jullian, the brilliant historian of ancient Gaul, has put the case for Vercingetorix with his customary eloquence: "Slowly, but without a false step and without an hour lost, his judgment sure, his resolution forearmed, impressing the weak with his awesome presence, the leaders with his logic, the

2.2   Coin of Vercingetorix

*ISS, 108-9; *Romans on the Rhine*, 77.

mob with his eloquence, the Gauls as a whole with his simple, unruffled courage; an adroit and fiery orator, a patient negotiator, order and method personified, undiscouraged in defeat, unassuming in victory, this extraordinary man taught the warriors of Gaul, in a few months, techniques and procedures completely foreign to their nature. He gave them discipline, self-mastery, perseverance in manual labor; he reconciled them to an unheroic strategy of attrition and hard work. He prepared them for victory before he let them seek it."

Vercingetorix advocated a policy of scorched earth and guerrilla warfare; it was against his better judgment that he undertook, in 52 B.C., the defense of Avaricum, capital of the Bituriges, now the cathedral city of Bourges. The town was surrounded by a nearly impenetrable network of streams and swamps, except on the southeast. Here Caesar built his camp. Its traces were discovered in 1887 by an English schoolmaster, who, enjoying the view from the cathedral tower, noticed roadbuilding going on to the southeast. Hastening to the spot, he found and sketched traces of Caesar's ditch in the chalky earth of the cutting for the road.

But Avaricum is better known for the elaborate siegeworks which Caesar was forced to build to capture it. The town was defended by a stout wall reinforced with beams in the Gallic manner (see model, Fig. 2.3). In front of the wall ran a deep ravine, which Caesar's men, working round the clock, filled in with crisscrossed ties to a total width of 330 feet. Upon these they erected sheds, to protect the men as they constructed wooden causeways on which to roll the 80-foot towers designed to overtop the Gallic wall. Parallel with the wall they built platforms, again with sheds on top to protect and conceal the legionaries before the final assault. The shed roofs were made of tile and covered with rawhide, to reduce the fire hazard, for the Gauls continually threw down upon them burning pitch and tallow. When the Romans tried to pull down the Gallic wall with hooks, the defenders ingeniously lassoed the hooks and pulled them in with windlasses.

2.3   Avaricum, siegeworks, model

They also built wooden towers, protected with hides, on their own wall, to equal the height and cancel the advantage of the Roman ones. Skilled in mining, they did their best to undermine the Roman siegeworks. But their bravery and ingenuity were in vain. After the siege had gone on for twenty-five days, Caesar took advantage of a torrential downpour to get his men onto the Gallic wall, encircling the defenders. The Romans were thirsting for vengeance for the massacre at Cenabum; in the end, only 800 out of 40,000 Gauls escaped, and all their grain and provisions fell into Caesar's hands.

Such was the magnetism of Vercingetorix' personality that the reverse only enhanced his prestige, and his next confrontation with Caesar was quite another story. The scene was Vercingetorix' native town, on the bleak plateau of Gergovia (Puy-de-Dôme), rising 2420 feet above sea level, 1200 feet above the plain, some eight miles south of Clermont-Ferrand. Napoleon III was persuaded to interest himself in the site by Prosper Mérimée, who, though best known as the librettist of *Carmen,* did yeoman duty, which he describes with modesty and wit, as an inspector in the archaeological service.

In 1862 the site was called Merdogne—which might euphemistically be translated as "Smellville." Napoleon III decreed that it should revert to its ancient name and receive a monument.* The indefatigable Stoffel worked at Gergovia; twenty-five years ago the oldest inhabitant could still remember how the Colonel's 300 workmen had made the dirt fly. They excavated Caesar's camps below the plateau, and placed markers described as "not false but casual." New excavation just before World War II confirmed the general accuracy of Stoffel's plan: Caesar's main camp cov-

---

*Another monument was dedicated in 1942, when Gallic resistance was again meaningful. The nineteenth-century monument in Clermont-Ferrand is by Bartholdi, the sculptor of the Statue of Liberty in New York harbor.

ered ninety acres, large enough for 20,000 men. It was not four-square in plan, but followed the contours of the terrain, as at Nointel. The recent excavators found sling and catapult bullets, a gate, a rampart in stone and mortar strong enough to break a plowshare, and the beginning of the double ditch leading to Caesar's smaller camp (seventeen acres, for 3,500–4,000 men) to the west. At the small camp, the new excavators found Stoffel's markers completely accurate: using them as landmarks for digging, they hit Caesar's ditch every time. This camp, too, was irregular in outline, following the contours; its ditch was double, and it had a palisade. No bullets were found; Caesar never mentions an attack upon this camp.

The Gallic oppidum atop the plateau was also excavated before World War II. It proved to have a double rampart, and there were coins and pottery of the period of Vercingetorix. The finds from the hundreds of houses are divided between the site museum and the one in Clermont-Ferrand. The excavators found a villa with mosaics and painted walls, a metalworker's shop and forge (as at Mt. Beuvray), and 350 sling-bullets. Gergovia held out against Caesar, inflicting upon him a loss of forty-six centurions and 700 men, so that he found it prudent to withdraw. The excavations show that Gergovia prospered "with surprising intensity" after the battle, and continued to be a place of pilgrimage, as its temples prove, down into the first Christian century.

Gergovia was the peak of Vercingetorix' success. Not surprisingly, it is the setting for one of an extremely witty and literate modern French cartoon series, in which the hero, Astérix, outwits the Romans every time.

While Caesar was being worsted at Gergovia, his faithful lieutenant Labienus was having better luck at Lutetia Parisiorum, which is what the Romans called Paris. Paris was never more than a prosperous small town in Roman times: the Romans fixed the capital of the Three Gauls (Aquitania, Belgica, Lugdunensis) more centrally, at Lugdunum (Lyon). The Gallic defender of

Paris, Camulogenus, burned his village on the Ile de la Cité, in order to deny it to Labienus, and broke down its bridges, which is why Paris has no archaeological remains of Gallic Lutetia. The details of the battle which Labienus won there are not clear; Caesar in defeat had no desire to point to the successes of his lieutenant. Labienus probably camped on the right bank, crossed the Seine at the Ile des Cygnes, within eyeshot of the present Eiffel Tower, and fought his battle on the plain which stretches toward Versailles. After the victory he hastened to rejoin his chief. The damage he inflicted was apparently not irreparable, for the Parisii were later able to send 8,000 men to help Vercingetorix.

The resistance leader had fortified and provisioned Alesia, nowadays Alise-Ste.-Reine, which was to prove to be the site of his last stand. The spot where the final tragic act of the drama of Gallic resistance was to be played out lies on the western edge of the Burgundy wine country, in a landscape of gentle slopes, fertile and shaded; the oppidum plateau, 1371 feet high and 222 acres in area, is bracketed north and south by the tree-lined rivers Oze and Ozerain; in the distance, fresh, misty hills; everywhere, nature smiling and at peace, in sharp contrast with the violence of the events of which this idyllic spot was once the theater. Here is one of the rare places where archaeology and history meet. We owe to Napoleon III the tracing on the ground of the plan of the immense and complicated siegeworks as described by Caesar. The emperor celebrated his connection with the place by erecting in 1865, at the west end of the plateau, a huge bronze statue of Vercingetorix, in Bronze Age armor but with fierce moustaches giving him some resemblance to his imperial patron (Fig. 2.4). The Emperor's agents were Colonel Stoffel and the local director of the excavations, Victor Pernet, who was among the first archaeologists to recognize cropmarks—lines of darker green in the fields, indicating where the ground has been disturbed by ancient trenches below. He recorded these lines with markers which still survive. The key to

2.4   Alésia, Vercingetorix statue

Caesar's scheme, as discovered by Pernet, is the double concentric ring of fortifications (see Stoffel's plan, Fig. 2.5): an inner one, the contravallation, to keep the Alesians in; and an outer one, the circumvallation, to keep the relieving force of Gauls out. The inner ring, nine miles in circumference, had a parapet, towers, a double ditch, and an elaborate system of "tank traps" (see model, Fig. 2.6). Nearest the ditch Caesar planted sharpened tree trunks, in interlaced rows of five, pointing toward the enemy. In modern warfare their function is served by barbed wire. Their nickname in Roman soldier slang was *cippi,* "tomb-

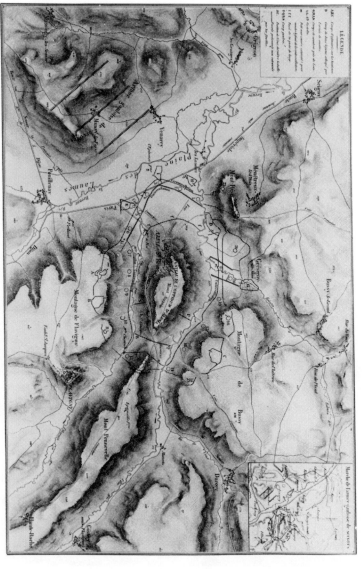

2.5   Alésia, plan of Caesar's siegeworks, commissioned by Napoleon III

2.6   Alésia, "tank traps," model

stones." Beyond them the soldiers dug eight diagonal rows of pits three feet deep and three feet apart, tapering toward the bottom, in which they imbedded sharpened and fire-hardened logs as thick as a man's thigh, and then covered the pits with twigs and brushwood. The soldiers called them *lilia,* "lilies": their function was to break the legs of the enemy horses. And beyond them came a thick crop of logs sprouting iron hooks called *stimuli,* or "goads". Samples of the Mark I and Mark II models of these are shown in Fig. 2.7.

The line of circumvallation was similar to the inner ring, but longer (nearly thirteen miles), and with only one ditch. Associated

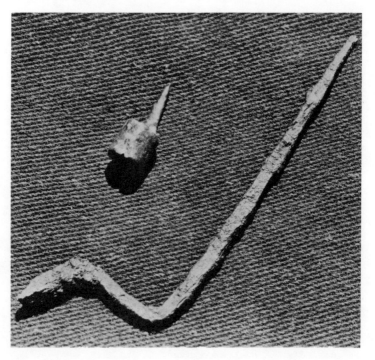

2.7   Alésia, *stimuli*

with these siegeworks were eight camps, identified by letters on Stoffel's plan, and twenty-three redoubts, indicated by numbers. It has been calculated that at the rate of a meter a day per man it would have taken 34,000 men a month to do all the digging required. To Caesar, it was worth the effort. The penned-in Gauls were being slowly starved to death. One of their number even proposed recourse to cannibalism, at the expense of those too young or too old to fight.* In the event, the non-combatants were not eaten but expelled, a fate perhaps even more cruel. The Gallic situation was desperate. Vercingetorix had 80,000 people in the town. A side of beef would feed 800, at half a pound per person; he needed forty-two tons of rations per day, and his water supply was in constant danger of pollution. The arrival of an immense relieving force of 245,000 Gauls, who camped on the slopes to the west of Caesar's lines (plan, lower left corner), heartened Vercingetorix' beleaguered forces, but not for long. Caesar defeated them, with enormous Gallic losses; thousands were caught on the goads or impaled on the lilies. Caesar records bitter fighting on the slopes of Mont Réa (northwest of Camp D on the plan). Caesar in his scarlet cloak hurried personally to the relief of Mont Réa. The Gauls were taken front and rear, and Vercingetorix abandoned hope and withdrew into Alesia. Pernet found the grim archaeological evidence of the bloody battle: some five cubic meters of bones of men and horses; daggers, armor, helmets, cuirasses, lances, swords, spearpoints, spurs, shield-bosses, ballista balls, and coins minted by at least twenty different Gallic tribes— which shows the width and variety of the response which Vercingetorix had succeeded in evoking. The fate of the defenders is symbolized in the tiny figure of a dead or dying Gaul found in an ancient cemetery of the town in 1906 (Fig. 2.8).

Finally the leader's countrymen handed him over to his enemy.

*For the elaborate fortifications and the cannibalism, compare the description of Scipio's siege of Numantia, *ISS*, 110-116.

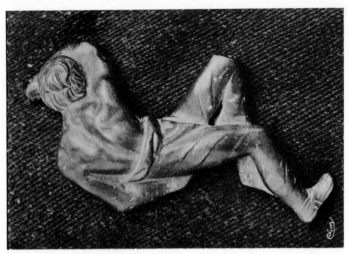

2.8   Alésia, dying Gaul, statuette

Caesar, who wanted to conciliate the Gauls, is extremely terse
about the event, but Plutarch describes it: the conqueror seated in
his proconsul's curule chair on a dais on the slopes of Mt. Fla-
vigny, surrounded by the standards of his legions; Vercingetorix
emerging alone, on horseback, tall, fierce, and proud in his
dress armor glittering with silver and enamel. He rode in a circle
around Caesar, then dismounted, flung down his arms and his
medals, and sat quietly at the feet of his conqueror. Caesar sent
him to Rome, kept him in prison for six years, displayed him in
his triumph, and then had him strangled.

We introduced Vercingetorix with the eloquence of a Frenchman, Camille Jullian. Let us bow him off the stage with the
stirring words of a British admirer, Theodore Rice Holmes: "In
him idealism was steadied by vision of the real; imagination was
served by mastery of detail; enthusiasm was sustained by resolution; the brain was fellow-worker with the heart. He fought to
make Gaul free by making her one, and what though this en-

deavour, almost successful, did ultimately fail? Gaul had to work
out her salvation in another way, because she was not ripe to obey
her leader's voice. To be great, and yet to fail, is tragical, but
Nature sees to it that her noblest children shall not waste their
strength. If Vercingetorix, like Hannibal, was the hero of a lost
cause, his influence also is inexhaustible. For the achievement is
less than the quest of the ideal, and no heroic deed was ever done
in vain."

Thirty-eight years after Rice Holmes wrote those words, the
survivors of another and more successful Gallic resistance set
up on the plain of Les Laumes below Alesia a marker which reads
(in translation):

1949
ON THIS PLAIN 2000 YEARS AGO
GAUL SAVED HER HONOR,
PITTING, AT VERCINGETORIX' CALL,
HER PEOPLES AGAINST CAESAR'S LEGIONS.
AFTER HER REVERSAL UPON THE BATTLEFIELD,
RECONCILED WITH THE VICTOR,
UNITED, DEFENDED AGAINST THE INVASIONS
OF THE GERMANS,
OPEN TO THE ENLIGHTENMENT OF GREECE AND ROME,
SHE KNEW THREE CENTURIES OF PEACE.

The truth behind this rhetoric has been revealed by the excavations of Alesia town. In the foreground of the air photograph
(Fig. 2.9), the theater, smaller than Pompeii's but larger than
those of Arles or Orange, dates from Alesia's prosperity in the
age of the Roman Emperor Vespasian (A.D. 69–79). Behind the
theater lay the basilica, with three apses, a smaller replica of Trajan's (A.D. 112) in Rome, and the Forum of about A.D. 150 (see
plan, Fig. 2.10). North of the Forum ran a porticoed street bordered with houses, of which one contained, in a crypt, a statue
of the Mother Goddess, with fruits in her lap; another was perhaps the clubhouse of the metalworkers of Alesia; a bronze vase

2.9   Alésia, air view of Gallo-Roman town

inscribed with the name of their patron, the god Ucuetis, was found in it. This same god secured for Alise-Ste.-Reine the honor of being Vercingetorix' Alesia. This title had been questioned by enemies of Napoleon III, who, not daring to oppose him politically, indicated their hostility by impugning him as an archaeologist. No less than seven other towns were advanced as *the* Alesia, but they were all discredited when Martialis' dedication to Ucuetis (Fig. 2.11) was found in Alise-Ste.-Reine, for its unmistakably names Alesia in the last line.

South of the Forum is the House of the Silenus, so called from a bronze weight found in it, bearing the likeness of the god, companion of Bacchus on his drunken sprees. In the courtyard well were found an iron-bound bucket and a Pan-pipe that would still play after over 1500 years of silence. The well also yielded egg-

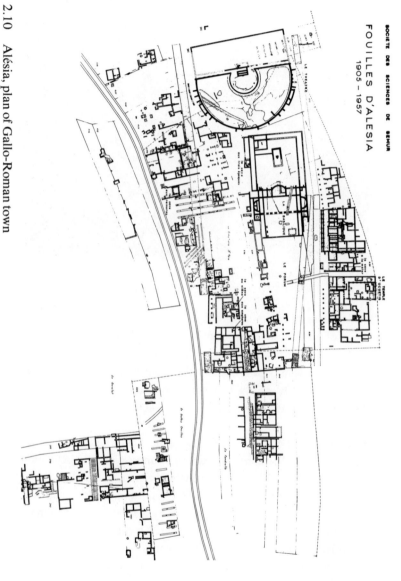

2.10   Alésia, plan of Gallo-Roman town

2.11   Alésia, Ucuetis inscription

shells, nuts, prune pits, shoe soles; and the well and the lower
levels of the house a plane, a pruning hook, two horseshoes, a
cowbell, hatchets, knives, and hundreds of nails. Coins showed
that the house was destroyed in the reign of Alexander Severus
(A.D. 222–235). Alesia had survived Caesar's victory for the
300 years recorded in the 1949 inscription.

After the fall of Alesia to Caesar, a pocket of Gallic resistance
held out at Uxellodunum, in central France. Caesar's lieutenant
Hirtius described the spot: a stronghold defended on all sides by
steep rocks, the only source of water for the defenders a spring,
which the Roman engineers diverted by a tunnel, and so forced
the town to surrender. The discovery of a man-made tunnel at
Puy-d'Issolu, which generally fits Hirtius' description, makes its
identification with Uxellodunum certain. Here too, as at Avaricum, the Roman engineers built a siege-terrace and a tower

(model, Fig. 2.12), and thus made the thirsty defenders capitulate. To make an example, Caesar ordered the right hands of all those who had borne arms to be cut off, and with this act the Gallic War was over. He followed conquest with conciliation, levying a moderate tribute, and loading the Gallic chiefs with presents. When he left Gaul, the following year, to fight Pompey for supremacy, the Gauls sent their bravest warriors to fight under his standard.

2.12   Uxellodunum, siegeworks, model

The French are a proud people, and the thought of Caesar's conquest has rankled. Jullian himself concluded that the Romans struck Gaul a mortal blow for her present, erased her past, and retarded her future. But this is overstated. As the 1949 plaque says, Rome protected Gaul, or strengthened her to protect herself, against the Germans. Alesia's later history, with its time-hallowed worship of Ucuetis and other native gods, is proof of how little Rome effaced Gaul's past. And as for the future, it was bright in every material way: in agriculture, metallurgy, ceramics, commerce. On the spiritual side, the Romans opened to the Gauls all the resources of Greek harmony, Roman reason, and, in time, Christian faith. If Vercingetorix had won, the Gallic common people would have been no better off: their own society granted them no voice in public affairs, and many of them, to escape death and taxes, entered into a voluntary servitude to Gallic masters which closely resembled serfdom.* Gallic unity, therefore, was precarious, and would probably not have outlived the resistance leader. If the Romans had withdrawn, Germans would have come in to fill the vacuum. To French patriots, this is never a cheerful prospect, so that the Roman conquest appears at the very least the lesser of two evils. But when we look, as we are now about to do, at the flourishing culture of cities which was the direct consequence of the Roman presence, the conquest seems more like a positive good.

*Caesar, *Gallic War*, 6.13, 1-2.

III

Augustan Cities

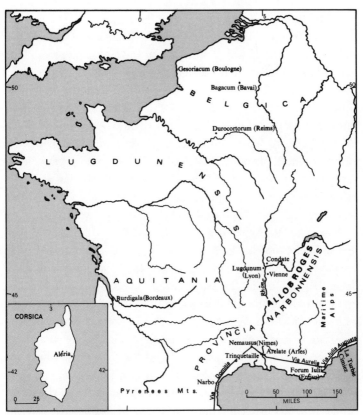

3.1   Map: Augustan Gaul

Placards carried in Caesar's triumph over Gaul in 46 B.C. recorded, with some exaggeration, 800 forts taken, 300 tribes subdued, a million dead, a million prisoners. The years of bloodletting were over; it was time to begin to bind up wounds. Caesar had already begun the work when the assassins' daggers struck him down. The task of organizing the newly-won territory therefore fell to his heir, Octavian-Augustus. Between 39 and 10 B.C. he was in Gaul four times, often for extended periods. The result was the military, administrative, economic, and religious settlement which we shall be examining in this chapter. He pacified the mountain tribes of the Pyrenees and the Maritime Alps, and set up a memorial to his accomplishment at La Turbie (see map, Fig. 3.1). He divided the territory Caesar had conquered into three provinces (for had not his predecessor written the immortal words, "All Gaul is divided into three parts"?): Lugdunensis, with its capital at Lugdunum (now Lyon); Aquitania, capital Burdigala (Bordeaux); and Belgica, whose capital was Durocortorum (Reims). He built roads, took the census, set up a system of tax-collection, and brought the Gauls into the Roman state religion by ordaining an annual meeting of the sixty Gallic tribes (*civitates*) at a new Altar of the Three Gauls at Lyon.

Above all, he founded or embellished cities. Before the Romans, Gallic oppida had been shabby and disorganized: the donkey was their city-planner. Now, the Romans encouraged those they set up as the Gallic ruling class to emulate Italian cities. Augustus himself was busy at this time turning Rome from a city of brick to a city of marble. This important aspect of Romanization meant that every respectable Gallic city would be ashamed not to possess most or all of the following, which we shall be describing in the sequel: a circuit wall, a regular grid plan, an amphitheater for gladiatorial shows, a theater, a civic center with a Forum for the transaction of business, a basilica for the law courts, a curia for the meetings of the town council, and a Capitolium for the worship of Jupiter, Juno, and Minerva;

sumptuous public bathing establishments; aqueducts and drains; the surrounding fields neatly centuriated (surveyed and alloted to Roman colonists and native Gauls); and a monumental arch celebrating, as Voltaire implied, the city's own subjection. This enhancement of the beauty of their towns, this rise in their living standards, was the consolation Rome offered the Gauls for the humiliation of their conquest. Most Gauls were grateful—grateful enough, in many cases, to pay for the beautification themselves—and the result was peace, prosperity, and a golden age.

The earliest Roman foundation in Gaul after the conquest was Arles, carved out of the territory of defeated Marseille in 46 B.C. by the father of the future Emperor Tiberius, as a colony for the veterans of the Sixth Legion (*Legio Sexta*) and christened *Colonia Julia Paterna Arelate Sextanorum*. Its most conspicuous Roman monuments (Fig. 3.2) are the theater, and the amphitheater, where gladiators once fought wild animals, and where bullfights can be seen to this day, which is appropriate when one remembers that the composer of *Carmen* also wrote *L'Arlésienne*. The amphitheater measures 446 by 351 feet, being halfway in size between the one in Pompeii and the Coliseum in Rome, and twentieth among the seventy known in the whole Roman world. It has a twin in Nimes, and we know the name of the architect, T. Crispius Reburrus—an unusual fact, since ancient architects' names are rarely handed down to posterity. The amphitheater at Arles has sixty arches on each of two levels, the lower framed with Doric half-columns, the upper with Corinthian. Pierced consoles on the upper level held the masts for the awning. The amphitheater would hold 21,000 to 25,000, with reserved seats (grooves in the stone show that the space allowance was sixteen inches) for members of certain religious sodalities, one devoted to the Gallic forest-god Silvanus, another to the Egyptian goddess Isis. Arles was a river port, and sailors were enthusiastic Isis-worshipers. The ship owners and the Maritime Union had their places, too, as did the

3.2   Arles, air view

town dignitaries. There are beast-cages under the arena, and finds
of antlers and boars' tusks show what beasts were fought there.
The amphitheater owes its extraordinary state of preservation
to the fact that it was used as living quarters and as a fortress dur-

ing the Middle Ages; two surviving medieval towers are visible in
the air photograph, and there were still houses in the arena in the
eighteenth century.

The date of the amphitheater is controversial. It is hard to believe that the veterans for whom the colony was founded could
have got along without a place for viewing blood-sports. But this
hypothetical first phase must have been in wood. The stone phase
involved the demolition of part of the circuit wall, not built till
16 B.C. Also, the amphitheater is oriented, not to the original
colonial grid, but to a new and later quarter. Futhermore, the
architectural décor is unfinished. The major Gallic event which
could have halted an important building project is the rebellion
of Vindex, in A.D. 68. This date is confirmed by a pottery dump
found under the arena, in which the sherds are dated in the latter
part of the first Christian century.

The theater is another and more humane gesture of the new
colony in the direction of Roman culture. Since, unlike the amphitheater, it is oriented with the original grid, it is presumably
of Augustan date; a statue of Augustus, and an altar to his patron
Apollo adorned the center of the stage building. Between the
orchestra and the permanent architectural backdrop behind the
stage was the slot into which the curtain was rolled down before
the start of a performance. The decoration throughout was
sumptuous. The orchestra was paved with green marble, trimmed
with red. The façade bore bulls' heads, the totem, so to speak, of
the Sixth Legion for whose veterans Arles was founded. Statues
abounded, including a Venus, found in 1651, presented to Louis
XIV, and now in the Louvre; a trio of Maenad dancers, and a
Niobid, part of a series illustrating characters of classical Greek
tragedy. The theater's size, too, is impressive: it is 334 feet in
diameter, and would hold 7,500 people, three times as many as
the Salle Pleyel in Paris, but not as many as the theaters of ancient Alesia, Lyon, or Vienne.

Modern Arles, a flourishing city of 30,000, overlies the ancient colony, and not much else that is Roman remains above ground. But west of the theater, beyond the cathedral, and under the Museum of Christian Art, lies a Roman underground structure of imposing dimensions, the cryptoporticus. It consists of three double, parallel tunnels, supported by fifty piers. The tunnels are arranged in the form of a U, measuring 200 by 400 feet in length, 28 feet in width, and over 14 feet to the top of their vaults. Since the walls are waterproofed, the tunnels must have served to store grain in transit to feed Rome; similar warehouses are known in Narbonne, Reims, and Bavai. The Arles cryptoporticus was built by Greeks (no doubt from Marseille), for Greek masons' marks are hacked on the stonework. A statue of Augustus and a replica of the shield voted to him in 26 B.C. by the Senate and People of Rome were found in the tunnels. The shield bears an inscription praising Augustus "for valor, clemency, justice, and piety to the gods and the fatherland." This warehouse lay under the Forum, and a temple, probably the Capitolium, lay just to the north of it; over its southeast corner today rises the Hôtel de Ville (City Hall) of modern Arles.

Before we leave Arles we should mention traces of the circus, for chariot races, by the river to the southwest, and the recent (1964) discovery, across the Rhône in the suburb of Trinquetaille, of a portico containing offices like those of the Piazzale delle Corporazioni at Ostia, the port of Rome*. And in the plain of Crau, east of the city, one can still see the boundaries of ancient centuriation, the surveyed allotments of plots of land which made the veterans of the Sixth Legion men of property.

Caesar could hardly have left his newly-conquered territory without a capital. He appointed his lieutenant, L. Munatius Plancus, governor of the new province, and it was no doubt in accordance with the murdered dictator's wishes that Plancus

*Mute Stones Speak, 260ff.

founded the capital of the Three Gauls in 43 B.C. at the confluence
of the Rhône and the Saône, and named it the *Colonia Copia
Felix Munatia Lugdunum*, now Lyon. Its main east-west street,
the *decumanus*, was oriented to coincide with sunrise on October
9, 43 B.C. Thanks possibly to the fact that former president Her-
riot of France was once mayor of Lyon, the city boasts the only
permanent archaeological dig in France. It has unearthed, along
with much else, a 1,000-foot stretch of the decumanus, granite-
paved, and thirty Roman feet wide. The decumanus is visible in
the model (Fig. 3.3), running just north of the theater (north is
to the right). The rectangle north of the decumanus is the Forum
of the colony, on the hill of Fourvière, a corruption of the Latin
Forum Vetus. Lyon's nineteenth-century cathedral lies over the
Capitoline temple which faced the Forum. Other Roman buildings on the model with which we shall be concerned are the Odeon
beside the theater, the new Forum and temple precinct to the
northwest, and the amphitheater and Altar of the Three Gauls
across the Saône. The river port was opposite the island, by the
bridge; on the island were workshops and warehouses. The center
of modern Lyon lies across the Rhône to the east, at the bottom
of the model; the Fourvière quarter is now a backwater, full of
fine Renaissance houses, picturesque except for the cathedral and
the adjoining television tower, which are a pair of eyesores.

The Forum of Lugdunum, measuring 460 by 200 feet, is com-
parable in size to the one at Alesia, and to the one at Augst in
Switzerland, also founded by Plancus, in the same year as Lyon*.
Lyon's Forum is of Augustan date, as shown by a hoard of 271
Augustan silver coins found in it. North of it rose the palace, where
the Emperors Augustus, Tiberius, Caligula, Vitellius, and Hadrian
lived, where Claudius and Caracalla were born, where the pre-
tender Albinus was murdered. But the square on which the palace
faced was not Lyon's original Forum; the substructure of that

*See Romans on the Rhine, 31.

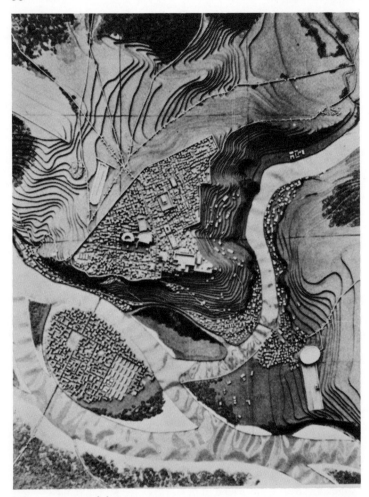

3.3   Lyon, model

was excavated between 1960 and 1965, in front of the theater. It is a U-shaped double portico, like the cryptoporticus at Arles; probably it was the basement of the courtyard of Plancus' headquarters. It was destroyed when the theater was built, between 16 and 14 B.C., during one of Augustus' stays in Gaul.

Ten thousand cubic meters of earth, lying seven meters deep, had to be removed to get at the theater. In its Augustan phase it was of modest proportions, smaller than Arles'. Its building stone was towed upriver in barges from Glanum, the blocks cut on the diagonal to save weight. Its present state, visible in the air photograph along with the Odeon (Fig. 3.4), represents a doubling in the number of seats, to 10,500, under Hadrian, in about A.D. 119. At that time the orchestra was paved with gray granite trimmed with red and green marble. The front four rows, wide and shallow, were planned to hold comfortable armchairs for 200 town dignitaries. The curtain slot was well enough preserved to make possible the construction of a working model, on display in the adjoining museum. The curtain was fastened in strips to a series of fifteen uprights ingeniously contrived to be moved up and down in fitted shafts by the operation of counterweights. Another set of counterweights wound the strips of cloth around drums in the bottom of the slot. A road, the pavement of which is visible, bordered the theater at the top. Facing the road was the sanctuary of Cybele, the great mother goddess of Asia Minor.

The sanctuary was identified and dated as long ago as 1704 by the discovery of an inscribed altar of A.D. 160; another, of 190, came to light in 1820; more recently a twice-life-size marble head of the goddess has been found. Her temple stood in a precinct measuring 170 by 282 feet, entered by a staircase and porch on the west, the side opposite the theater. On the east, above the theater and visible in the air photograph, rose a podium supporting the cella in which the goddess' statue had stood. In the middle of the precinct was an altar; around it were shops where religious objects were sold. The existence of the sanctuary, where most of the worshipers must have been Asiatics, shows how cosmopolitan Lyon had become the two hundred years since its founding.

To the south of the theater, the air photograph shows a smaller building, the Odeon, built in a technique exactly like that of the

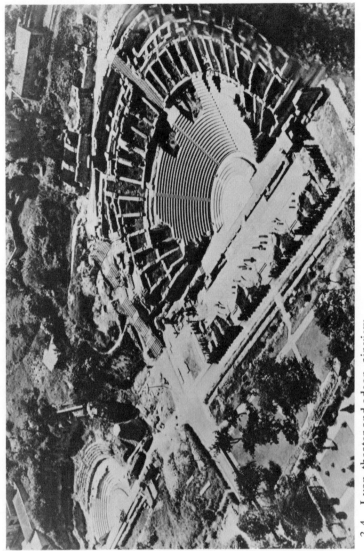

3.4   Lyon, theater and odeon, air view

Cybele sanctuary, and therefore to be dated, like it, at about A.D.
160. An Odeon was a covered auditorium, used for music or lectures. Such buildings are rare in Gaul; the only other is in Vienne.
The one in Lyon held three thousand people. We may be sure it
was roofed, because the bearing walls are over twenty feet thick.
It was richly decorated, using eleven different kinds of stone, imported from all over the Empire, in eight colors: gray, black, violet, green, yellow, peach, pink, and red. The excavator, with pardonable pride, describes the orchestra paving, with its colorful
patterns of squares, rectangles, lozenges, and circles, as the most
beautiful of the ancient world. Neglected during World War II,
the Odeon crumbled from sixteen rows of seats to a mass of
rubble. The orchestra paving was originally set in cement. The
modern restoration is based upon the fragments of marble of different colors found adhering to it. The restored Odeon is used
in the summer for plays and concerts, including rock-and-roll,
which there is some reason to suspect the ancient Lyonnais would
have enjoyed, too.

The other major building of Lyon visible above ground is the
amphitheater, on the hillside of Croix-Rousse, across the Saône to
the northeast of the ancient civic center, where the old Gallic
oppidum of Condate had been. Here, during the celebration of
Lyon's 2000th anniversary in 1958, a tablet was discovered, in
use face down as the cover of a well. The tablet bore an almost
complete inscription (Fig. 3.5) giving the date of the amphitheater
—the equivalent of A.D. 19—and the name of the donor, a Gallo-
Roman from Saintes called C. Julius Rufus, who records that he
was a priest of Rome and Augustus.* The donor's ancestors had
Celtic names: he is the type of Gallic aristocrat who felt his for-

---

*Augustus was deified after his death, which shows how irreligious the
Romans were, and also foreshadows how far down the road to absolutism
the empire would go before its fall.

3.5   Lyon, amphitheater inscription

tune linked to Rome's; such men were among the main agents of
Romanization.

The amphitheater served as the meeting place for the council
of the sixty Gallic tribes; seats inscribed with the names of some
of them were found by the excavators. Under Hadrian, between
130 and 136, the amphitheater was enlarged from 341 feet in
length to 459, which made it larger than those of either Arles or
Nimes. Before that, it had been used for oratory competitions.
The Emperor Caligula, whose bouts of insanity had their lucid
intervals, made it a rule when he visited Lyon in A.D. 40 that the
losers should either erase their effusions with their tongues or be
ducked in the Rhône. In 177 the amphitheater was the scene of
St. Blandina's martyrdom, brought on by the devotees of Cybele,
incensed that Christian Easter conflicted with the date of initia-
tion into their mysteries. Blandina and the other victims were
mauled by wild beasts, beheaded, and their corpses thrown into
the Rhône.

East of the amphitheater, in a huge rectangular precinct approached by ramps (see model), Augustus' stepson Drusus dedicated, in 12 B.C., the Altar of the Three Gauls, by which the Ro-

man rulers hoped to link the old native religion to the official
Roman cult. The site was wooded, so that Druids, who worshiped
in forests, would feel at home. Fine houses for priests and dele-
gates adjoined. The altar was decorated with oak-leaf swags in
bronze appliqué. It bore the dedication ROMAE ET AVGVSTO, and
the names of the sixty tribes, whose symbolic statues stood in the
precinct. At the altar's corners stood thirty-two-foot columns of
gray Egyptian marble, bearing winged Victories in gilt bronze.
Only an unreconstructed Gallic patriot would think of the Victories as symbolizing Rome's conquest of Gaul, which already
lay forty years in the past when the altar was dedicated. Augustus
meant the statues to be interpreted as symbolizing his victory
over Antony and Cleopatra at Actium, in 31 B.C., which according to his propaganda unified the whole empire under his benign
principate. The precinct also contained statues of priests, and, at
the end nearest the amphitheater, a crematorium for the corpses
of gladiators killed in the arena. In 1524, near the site of the
altar, the famous and handsome bronze inscription was found
which bears the text of a speech made in A.D. 48 to the Roman
Senate by the Emperor Claudius (who, as we saw, was born in the

capital), advocating the entrance of Gauls into that august body. In 1969 the inscription was on display in the museum near the Roman theater.

Lyon, conceived by Caesar, embellished by Augustus and his successors, had in its prime a population of 50–80,000—nowadays it has over half a million. It was a social, political, religious, commercial, artistic organism, its streets, squares and alleys pulsing with life, with people going about their business peaceably. Roman Gaul was not troubled by violence in the streets. In the high empire an urban cohort of 1,200 men stationed in Lyon sufficed to keep the whole of Gaul in order. The Roman road net connected Lyon with the Channel and Atlantic ports, with the Rhine, with Narbonne, and Marseille. In the suburbs were luxurious villas with central heating, frescoed walls, and in rooms for gourmet dining, mosaic floors. Over a hundred mosaics have been unearthed in Lyon. Four aqueducts supplied villas and city with water. Inscriptions and graffiti, some unprintable, bring the ancient Lyonnais to life. They were a cosmopolitan lot. In the city's prime 30 percent of them had Greek names. They enjoyed the simple pleasures; one touching epitaph reads, in translation: "You who read this, go and bathe at the baths of Apollo, as I used to do with my wife, and would still, if I could." All this pleasant, civilized life came to an end in about A.D. 360, when barbarian invaders cut the aqueducts. The evidence for Lyon's fall comes partly from the pathetic hoards of coins, buried in panic and never recovered by their owners; from some such fragments as a hollow marble helmet from the detachable head of an Emperor's statue. Favored by nature, developed by man, Lyon in its prime had a triple glory, as Roman capital, as Gallic center, as Christian metropolis. Caesar chose the site well: Lyon revived, to become, as it is today, the second city, and, so the Lyonnais say, the gastronomic capital, of France.

Augustus, after his naval victory over Antony and Cleopatra at Actium, had 300 captured vessels on his hands. He decided to

send them to a port on the Provençal coast of France, Forum
Julii, nowadays Fréjus. The full name of the place was *Forum Iulii
Octavanorum Colonia Pacensis Classica;* this shows that it
was a colony of the Eighth Legion (*Legio Octava*), that Augustan
propaganda presented the place as a symbol of peace, and that it
was a naval base (*classica,* from *classis,* fleet). The artificial harbor, which covered fifty-four acres, is now filled in, and travelers
pass over it in the train between Marseille and Nice. It had a light-
house in its southwest corner, and its entrance was flanked by
towers and controlled by a chain-boom. Adjoining were a navy
yard, with warehouses and arsenal; also two fortified camps, with
towers, cisterns, grain-stores, baths, a barracks laundry, and elegant living quarters with mosaic floors, perhaps for the admiral.
The town itself, covering just under a hundred acres, was protected by a two-mile wall eight feet thick, and had the usual grid
of streets; the decumanus was the Via Aurelia, the highway from
Italy to Arles. The gate at its west end, the Porte des Gaules, was
cleared of excrescences by a flood in 1959, and now may be seen
to good advantage. The same flood improved the looks of the
amphitheater, about half the size of the one at Arles, measuring
370 by 269 feet; it would have held about 12,000 spectators.
Experts date this phase not earlier than Vespasian's reign in A.D.
69–79, because of the brick construction of its arches, but there
may well have been an Augustan phase in wood.

Like any self-respecting colony, Fréjus also had a theater,
with its seats facing south, to protect its occupants from the Provençal north wind, the mistral. It is too poorly preserved to allow
an estimate of its capacity, but its diameter is only four-fifths that
of the theaters of Arles and Lyon. The simplicity of its construction suggests that it dates from the foundation of the colony. Not
far from the theater, at the Porte de Rome, the town's aqueduct
enters. Its source is in the hills twenty-five miles to the northeast,
and its course can be traced by a number of its arches still standing in the countryside. The aqueduct served the town baths, of
which one arch, the Porte Dorée, of the third Christian century,

survives. Fréjus, then, had all the amenities with which the Romans regularly equipped their towns. What makes it unique in Gaul is the evidence of its combined military and civil function as an Augustan naval base. Boulogne is another example, but it was founded later, in A.D. 43, by Claudius for his invasion of Britain, and no Roman remains survive.

Augustus and his lieutenant Agrippa have left their mark particularly clearly on Nemausus, the present Nimes. The town took its name from a native water god, to whose healing spring Gauls had come for the cure long before the Romans. The site of the spring, landscaped in baroque style in 1740, is still, as the Jardin de la Fontaine, one of the most attractive quarters of the modern city. An inscription of 25 B.C., found near the spring, shows that the sanctuary was in use in Augustus' reign, but its most impressive remains are later. A U-shaped double portico was built in the second or third Christian century, with its open side facing the spring; a temple to Nemausus adorned its edge and a temple to Rome and Augustus stood in a central (axially symmetrical) position at the back of the portico; in the open space between the arms of the U there was an altar in the midst of a smaller portico, facing the kind of statue-ornamented fountain house which the Romans called a *nymphaeum*. The best-preserved and most interesting building, the "Temple of Diana" (see Fig. 8.20), opens off the west arm of the U. Part of its barrel-vaulted roof survives, and its walls have shallow statue-nitches. Parallels for its architectural style come from the reign of Hadrian, A.D. 117-138. Some archaeologists think that the temple, or the rooms adjoining it on either side, served as a dormitory where believers slept in the hope the goddess would visit them in the night with a miraculous cure.

From the site of a small theater at the north end of the east portico a flight of steps up to the most striking remnant of Nimes' circuit wall, the Tour Magne. The town's perimeter, over three and a half miles, enclosed nearly 500 acres; an inscription from one of its gates shows it to be Augustan, built in 16 B.C. Of the nineteen of its towers now known, the Tour Magne is the most impressive, a brick-faced octagon 130 feet high, in three setback stories. It may have served as a signal tower, a memorial of victory, or both. Its present state would be even more impressive had it not been for the notorious Provençal astrologer Nostradamus (1503–1566). In 1601 a local gardener conceived the notion that the tower concealed a fabulous fortune. Having read in Nostradamus a prophecy that a gardener would discover a treasure hidden in the earth, he obtained from Henry IV permission to excavate, which was revoked just in time to save the tower from total destruction. The treasure was never found, and the gardener returned to cultivating his garden.

Among the buildings which the circuit wall was built to protect is one of the best-known and best-preserved Roman temples in France, the Maison Carrée (Fig. 3.6). It stood on the south side of the Forum, a rectangular piazza measuring 460 by 230 feet, with the curia, where the town council met, to the north. Like the Forum, the temple's length and breadth (86 by 43 feet) are related in the proportion of two to one, and its 50-foot height was proportionally divided: podium 10 feet high, Corinthian columns 30 feet, superstructure, 10 feet. Its architrave (the marble beam running above the columns) was decorated on three sides with carved rosettes and acanthus leaves, the same lettuce-like foliage which, in three dimensions, inspired the Corinthian capital. The front originally had an inscription in bronze cut-out letters. The put-holes for attaching the letters are visible in the photograph. From them it has proved possible to restore the text of the inscription, and to show that the temple was dedicated twice: once by Agrippa, to Rome and Augustus, in 16 B.C., and again in A.D. 1, to Augustus' grandchildren, Lucius and Gaius, whose temple at Glanum was described above. The earlier dedication makes the Maison Carrée one of the earliest monuments

3.6 Nimes, Maison Carrée

of Roman ruler cult in western Europe. It has had a checkered
history, having served as an assembly hall, a house, a stable, a
church, a granary, the seat of the prefecture, and now as a mu-

seum. About 1670 Louis XIV's finance minister wanted to move it to Versailles, but local architects persuaded him it would not stand the journey. It has its relevance to America: in 1785 Thomas Jefferson, then Minister to France, had a stucco model made of it which inspired the State House still standing in Richmond, Virginia.

Some 400 yards southeast of the Maison Carrée, near the city wall, looms the amphitheater. Fig. 3.7 shows how nearly it is the twin to the one in Arles.

3.7   Nimes, amphitheater

The water-god's city needed more water than his spring could provide. Agrippa brought it from the river Gard, thirty miles away, in such quantity as to provide 400 liters of water per person per day; nowadays, 300 is considered enough. The arches of the Pont du Gard (Fig. 3.8) by which both road and water conduit crossed the river, make up one of the best-preserved, most picturesque, and most famous sections of aqueduct in the

3.8   Pont du Gard

Roman world. It stands 160 feet high, and visitors who do not suffer from acrophobia can still walk 900 feet along the top, on the slabs under which the water channel ran. The road ran above the lowest arches. The projecting stones visible in the photograph were left on purpose to support scaffolding for repairs. Some of the blocks weigh as much as six tons; they were laid without mortar, the courses being held together with iron clamps. Useful, civilizing public works of this kind go a long way toward justifying the Romanization of Gaul.

Nowadays from Nimes you can put your automobile on a plane for Corsica. The island was not administered with Gaul in Roman times, but since it now forms part of the same archaeological "circonscription" as Provence, it is appropriate to describe a Augustan foundation there, of 24 B.C., the *Colonia Veneria Julia Pacenis Restituta Aleria,* nowadays simply Aleria, halfway down the east coast, conveniently midway on the voyage from Marseille to Naples. Its history goes back to 565 B.C., when Greeks from Phocaea in Asia Minor planted a colony there, which they called Alalia. Carthaginians ousted them around 535; Rome ousted the Carthaginians in 231, and made Corsica one province with Sardinia. The left-wing general Marius, whom we have met before in Gaul, founded a colony twenty-seven miles north of Aleria at an uncertain date; his victorious opponent Sulla settled some veterans at Aleria itself in 81 B.C.; and Caesar did the same in 46. Its Forum, carefully excavated (Fig. 3.9) has an Augustan phase, as well as buildings dated before and after Augustus. It is in the shape of a trapezoid widening from east to west. At the east end is the temple, its dimensions 56 by 36 Roman feet, built in the technique called *opus incertum* (irregular, fist-size stones set in cement), which was current in the age of Sulla. The open space of the Forum, stretching west from the temple, was paved in green schist, and had a portico on the north and south sides. At the west end of each arm of the portico is a small

3.9   Aleria, air view

building of Caesarian date: it has been conjectured that the
south building was the office of the aedile (mayor). West of it are
the foundations of an Augustan arch; another arch, of Caesar's
time, faces the north building. Closing the west end of the Forum
is a large complex, built under Augustus, and arranged around a
porticoed court. It was identified as a *praetorium* (military headquarters), with a tribunal at the back, and a room where the
military standards might have been displayed; but more recently
it has been conjectured that the building could have been an
atrium publicum, containing offices, and facilities for entertaining official guests, as at Cosa in Etruria. North of it were Augustan
baths, with mosaic floors and shops. Northwest of the baths was
an industrial establishment of the first century B.C., near which a
vast quantity of oyster shells was found. They may have been

used for making *garum*, the fish-sauce so much relished by ancient gourmets. They possibly mark the site of the kitchen of the praetorium or atrium publicum.*

It was while visiting Corsica on archaeological business in 1840 that Prosper Mérimée collected the local color for his masterpiece, *Colomba*. Mérimée also, in line of duty, visited Vienne, on a curve of the Rhône, seventeen miles south of Lyon. It was the old capital of the Allobroges, who revolted against Rome and were punished by Mark Antony. He planted a colony of veterans there in 43 B.C. Under Augustus it became the *Colonia Julia Augusta Florentia Vienna*. It boasted a circuit wall with the longest perimeter of any in Gaul: over four miles, enclosing 544 acres, about half the area of Republican Rome itself. Augustus built for it (Fig. 3.10) the second largest theater in Gaul, the largest being at Autun. The theater at Vienne seated 10,800, and had a diameter of 354 feet, about the same as Augustus' Theater of Marcellus in Rome. Its excavation (1922-1938) required the removal of 80,000 cubic meters of earth; the completion of the work was celebrated by a performance in the restored theater of *The Damnation of Faust*, Berlioz having been a native of Vienne. The theater was planned on a Greek module, the cubit—the distance from the elbow to the fingertips. The best seats, in the first four rows, were of pink breccia and white marble, with griffin feet. As in Pompey's theater in Rome, there was a temple at the back, this one dedicated to Augustus' patron god, Apollo. The orchestra was paved with half-cubit blocks of yellow and pink stone. The stage, three cubits high, was faced with a forty-eight-cubit frieze of animals: lions, panthers, bulls, stallions, mastiffs, and goats. Dionysus, the Roman Bacchus or Liber, patron god of the drama, presided over the whole. There is a curtain slot, in which lead counterweights were found. Finds of coins show that

*See *ISS*, 207-210.

3.10 Vienne, theater

the theater was in use down to the time of Arcadius, A.D. 395-408. Vienne also has an Odeon, within a meter of being the same size as the one in Lyon. It is the only town in Gaul with three theaters. The third was devoted to mystery plays connected with the cult of Cybele. Her temple adjoins, and there is an underground room divided by nine columns into a nave and two side aisles; it contains basins where the faithful could wash after bathing in the blood of the sacred bull. Pottery found in the lowest level is of the mid-second century B.C. This Near Eastern cult complex is so far unique in the west.

Vienne also had a circus, for chariot races. It was 1492 feet long; its center (*spina*) is marked to this day by an obelisk ("La Pyramide"), adjoining which is Mme. Point's restaurant, considered by many gourmets to be the finest in France.

The best-preserved Roman monument in Vienne is the temple of Augustus and Livia (Fig. 3.11), nearly the twin of the Maison Carrée in Nimes. Like the Maison Carrée, it has a double inscription, showing that it was originally dedicated to Rome and Augustus. The later addition of the name of Augustus' wife Livia was made in A.D. 41 by the Emperor Claudius: she was his grandmother, and he declared her a goddess.

Recent excavations across the river, in the suburb of St.-Romain-en-Gal and in the city, have turned up ten mosaics. One, showing athletes throwing the discus, running, boxing, and wrestling, was on display at the 1968 Winter Olympics at Grenoble.

Another town with a modest claim to athletic distinction (because of its amphitheater) was Cemenelum, nowadays Cimiez, a former Ligurian oppidum above Nice. The amphitheater, its best known Roman building (Fig. 3.12), is one of the smallest in the Roman world, measuring only 220 by 184 feet. In its first phase it dates from the reign of Augustus, not long after 14 B.C. It seated about 500 in the best seats, and 2,500 more in the back. As in the

3.11   Vienne, temple of Augustus and Livia

3.12 Cimiez, amphitheater

theater at Emerita in Spain,* there was no intercommunication between classes and masses: the latter reached their seats by wooden
stairs from the outside. Small amphitheaters like this have their
parallels in Caerleon and Caerwent in Wales, and in Carnuntum
in Austria: these were camp areas, in which the class distinction
in seating was between officers and men. Cemenelum became a
garrison town, which developed south of the amphitheater. A
Roman building called the "Temple of Apollo", freed of a modern

*ISS, 137.

farmhouse built in its midst, proved to be a set of three baths, of the second and third Christian centuries. In the northernmost a statue of Antonia was found; she was a daughter of Mark Antony, wife of Augustus' stepson Drusus, and mother of the Emperor Claudius. These baths had exercise grounds: a stadium for footraces and a palaestra for wrestling. South of them ran the decumanus. Of the other two baths, the eastern was for men, and the western—in which an earring was found—for women; between them ran the *cardo*, the main north-south street. The latest coins were minted in the reign of the anti-Christian Emperor Julian the Apostate, A.D. 361–363. Thereafter, ironically, the women's baths became a Christian church, with the baptistery in the furnace room. The whole area, in the heyday of the empire, was a vast monumental complex, not without elegant houses, built to take advantage of the cool air and the view down upon Nice and the Côte d'Azur.

Above the Côte d'Azur, eleven miles east of Nice, at the Italian border, nearly 1600 feet up, stands La Turbie, the last and one of the most impressive Augustan monuments to be considered in this chapter. Its name, a corruption of the Latin *tropaeum*, defines its function: it is a trophy of Augustus' victory over forty-four Alpine tribes, named in the inscription on the face of the monument (Fig. 3.13), which bears a date corresponding to 6 B.C. Augustus, imitating the trophy (no longer extant) of Caesar's rival Pompey in the Pyrenees, also built his at the top of a pass, as a symbol of the pacification of Gaul. In Saracen times it became a fort, in the fifteenth century a castle keep, in the sixteenth a watchtower. In the eighteenth century it was blown up, and a village was built from its stones. In our own time an American philanthropist named Tuck subsidized its reconstruction as a symbol of unity and peace. The job was finished in 1933, the year Adolph Hitler came to power in Germany.

The 3,000 fragments which went into the reconstruction came

3.13   La Turbie, Trophy of Augustus

from thirty-two demolished houses of the village, which yielded
column capitals, shafts, and bases; building blocks, of local stone
and Carrara marble; moldings, bits of inscription, frieze, tro-

phies, statues, doors, niches, pediments, stair-treads; the circular
base of the statue of Augustus which had surmounted the whole,
161 feet above ground level; and the steps of the pyramid on
which the statue had stood.

The original architect had conceived the monument after the
model of Augustus' Mausoleum in Rome, which in turn had been
inspired in part by one of the seven wonders of the ancient world,
the Mausoleum at Halicarnassus.* Its plan works out a symbolic
exercise in solid geometry. The base is a cube, as solid as Augustus' victory; it bears the inscription with the names of the conquered tribes, and the trophies of arms captured from them. On
the cube rests a cylinder; a circular colonnade with niches at the
back for the statues of the lieutenants who, all equally, had
helped Augustus to win his victory, among them his stepsons,
Tiberius, who succeeded him, and Drusus. On the cylinder
rested a pyramid, rising in twelve steps to the statue, twice life-
size, of the godlike victor. The whole is planned to propagandize
the emperor's glory. The inscription and trophies are on the well-
lighted west face, at a point where three roads meet. The trophies
include kneeling captives, captured arms, the cloaks of the conquering generals. Among these, memorialized in the statues on
the second level, were not only the members of the dynast's im-
mediate family but also those who were more or less his partisans,
including the one with whom he used to play at dice, one who
proposed for him the title Father of his Country, and one who
was executed for conspiracy before the monument was finished.
The *appearance* of solidarity was what mattered; by 6 B.C. no one
would have been rash enough to question the reality, especially
with the Prince of Peace towering like a god at the top of the
whole political structure.

La Turbie remains what it was in the beginning, a symbol of

*Greek Stones Speak, 319-321; paperback, 295-297.

Augustus. Later ages have variously assessed the value of that symbol. To the Victorians, living in an empire made in the image of Rome, Augustus seemed a prototype of their own beneficent Queen; they would see nothing amusing in the comparison. To the liberals of the 1930's, living in the shadow of dictatorship, he was the forerunner of Hitler and Mussolini. To an age like ours, in which some question, in ignorance, the Roman tradition of liberty under law, Augustus may appear in a new light, as having supplied to a sick society the internal peace it so sorely needed. The Golden Age of Augustus was not merely a propaganda trick; it was a reality. Creative geniuses like Vergil and Horace do not flourish under mere pinchbeck dictators. In Rome and in Gaul men were genuinely grateful to Augustus. Enjoying the amenities and security of Augustan Arles, Lyon, Vienne, and the rest, they were hardly likely to sigh for a vanished Vercingetorix.

IV

The Fruits of Romanization

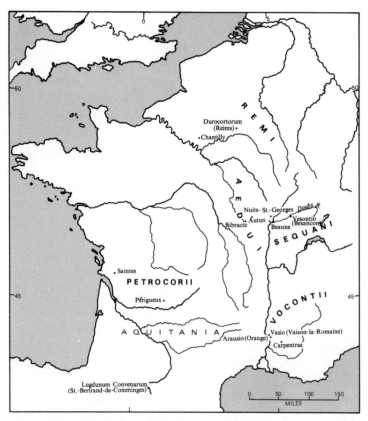

4.1　Map: Gallic sites of the high Empire

91

It took the Romans some seventy-five years, from Caesar's conquest in 51 B.C. to well on in the reign of Tiberius (A.D. 26-27), to get over their inferiority complex about the Gauls. The archaeological evidence for that complex is the number of monuments in which their trophies boast of victory. La Turbie was not the first: an earlier one was discovered in 1926 at Lugdunum Convenarum, nowadays St.-Bertrand-de-Comminges (see map, Fig. 4.1), in the foothills of the Pyrenees, where, as we have seen, Pompey had settled refugees from Spain. This settlement (72 B.C.), of which no remains have been found, was probably on the site of the Gallic oppidum, on a rocky outcrop high over the Garonne valley, 1463 feet above sea level, where the cathedral and the site museum now stand. There is a distant view of the Pyrenees rising into the blue, and a nearer vista of white houses with red tile roofs, nestled among the cypresses.

The findspot of the trophy was in the plain below, where Caesar or Augustus had laid out a gridded town. For forty years excavation was carried out here, often with his own hands, on a starvation budget, by a dedicated Gascon schoolmaster-archaeologist, born nearby, speaking the local dialect, and linked by blood or friendship with most of the owners of the land he wanted to excavate. His name was Bertrand Sapène. Looking out of his classroom window one day in 1926, he noticed a spot where sparse vegetation suggested Roman remains below ground. The place where he dug turned out to be between the Forum and the back of the temple of Rome and Augustus (see plan, Fig. 4.2). He found a pavement, a flat-topped mass of masonry on which statues might have rested, and a heap of statue-fragments which had been piled up in antiquity to feed a limekiln. So savage had been the destruction that it took as many as thirty fragments to restore a single statue. When the reconstruction was finished, with the help of experts from Paris, what emerged was a trophy arranged on three bases. On the central one, higher and wider than the other two, was a female Triton riding on the prow of a ship,

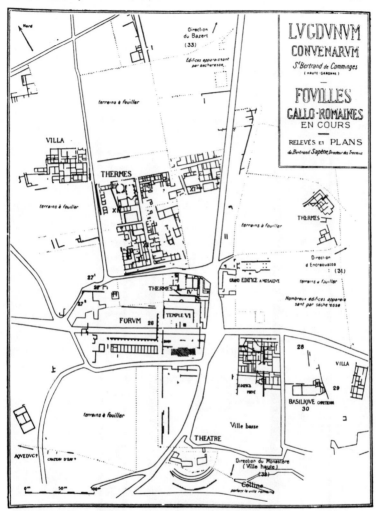

4.2a   St.-Bertrand-de-Comminges, plan

a globe, and an eagle. The group was probably flanked by a pair
of winged Victories, of which one was found. On either side of
the central naval motif was a pair of figures, one male, one female,

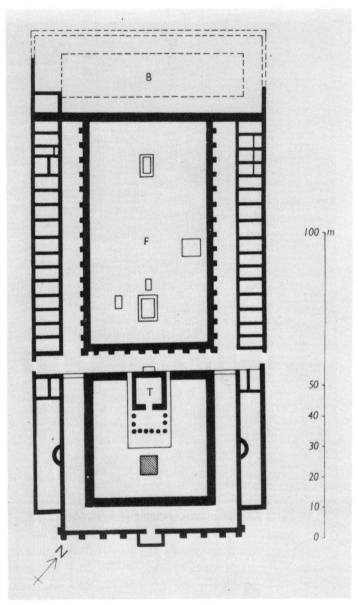

4.2b   St.-Bertrand-de-Comminges, Forum plan

chained to tree trunks. One of the females wore the Gallic torque; the other (Fig. 4.3), probably represented conquered Spain*; her melancholy expression suggests in the sculptor more empathy

ISS, Fig. 7.4.

4.3   St.-Bertrand-de-Comminges, Hispania, statue

with victim than with victor. The kneeling male figure (Fig. 4.4)
is also sympathetically rendered, tensed to his very toes in revolt
and refusal to accept defeat. This combination—naval victory,
conquered Spain, conquered Gaul—would have been most topi-
cal in the reign of Augustus, who won his naval victory over
Antony and Cleopatra at Actium in 31 B.C., and organized the
conquered Spaniards and Gauls from 27 to 25, spending
some time taking the waters to cure his arthritis in this very area
in 25. This is therefore the favored date for this trophy, though
Sapène pointed out that the local marble of which the sculptures
are made was not generally in use that early.*

The figures of the trophy faced the Forum, with their backs to
the temple of Rome and Augustus, which was almost the twin in
size to the Maison Carrée in Nimes and the temple of Augustus
and Livia in Vienne. The temple stood at the back, or west end,
of a precinct whose entrance was adorned with three statues: of
Trajan, of his wife Plotina, and of a local worthy, C. Julius
Serenus, a typical Romanized Gaul of the upper class, who, after
serving under Trajan as an officer in the East, returned to his native town, served as mayor and priest of Rome and Augustus, and
distinguished himself as a public benefactor. He may have donated
the small amphitheater, seating 5,000, which Sapène excavated
north of the town.

The age of Trajan (A.D. 98-117) was the heyday of Lugdunum
Convenarum. The town was on the main road from Toulouse to
the west, and was the point of collection of customs on goods from
Spain. Its circuit wall enclosed 338 acres, only one-third excavated; its population of perhaps 20,000 prospered from the mines,
quarries, fertile fields, pastures, and forests; from tourist-patients
bound, like Augustus, for the therapeutic bathing-resorts; and
from business men traveling to and from Spain. It also harbored,

---

*It supplied some material for Trajan's column in Rome (A.D. 112/3), and
for Louis XIV's palace at Versailles.

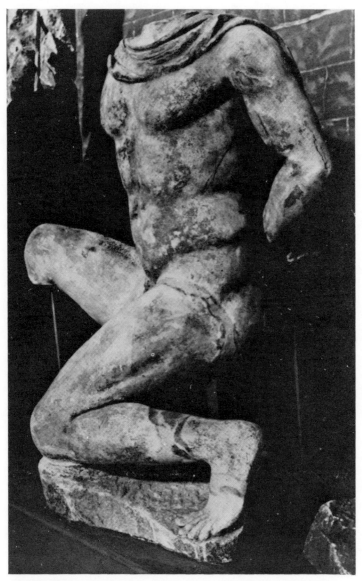

4.4   St.-Bertrand-de-Comminges, crouching Gaul, statue

from A.D. 39 on, a pair of famous exiles: Herod Antipas, to whom
Pilate had sent Christ to be tried, and Herod's wife Herodias; con-
demning their marriage caused the death of John the Baptist
(Herodias was Herod's niece). Caligula exiled Herod for claiming
the kingship, and his wife voluntarily shared his fate.

Sapène excavated the market-basilica, northeast of the Forum,
with its vast, 5,812-square-foot Augustan mosaic floor, its three
Trajanic apses, and its row of north and south shops of Antonine
date, ca. A.D. 150, these three phases testifying to over 150 years
of prosperity.

Like other prosperous Gallo-Roman towns, Lugdunum Convenarum had its aqueduct, still in places rising to a height of
twenty-six feet, which served two sets of public baths, equipped
with swimming pool, exercise grounds, massage rooms, and shops.
Where the ground rises toward Pompey's citadel, at the south end
of the cardo, rose the theater, about half the size of the one at
Arles, with rock-cut seats and a curtain slot.

The patrons of this theater, independent Gascons with names
like Belexco and Anderexo, kept their native cult. The local museum boasts 200 votive altars, and there are twice as many inscriptions to native as to Roman deities. But they also early
welcomed Christianity: a fourth-century church has been excavated, yielding twenty-eight sarcophagi, primitive terracotta
heads of Christ, and an inscription: DA, CHRISTE, FAMVLAE TVAE
AEMILIANAE REQVIEM ET VITAM AETERNAM. Aemiliana was
lucky to find her peace in the next world: in A.D. 408 the city was
deliberately and implacably Vandalized.

Another example of Roman gloating over vanquished Gauls
is to be seen in a relief (Fig. 4.5) on the east face of the arch of
Colonia Julia Minimorum Carpentorate, nowadays Carpentras,
fifteen miles southeast of Orange; in the seventeenth century the
local Palais de Justice was built against it. Two muscular Gallic
captives in fringed cloaks, one clad in a sheepskin, are chained

4.5   Carpentras, arch, detail

to a tree-trunk festooned with swords, war trumpets, and Gallic
helmets hanging from the ends of the branches like huge acorns.
At the top of the tree is the fringed bottom half of a cuirass; at
the bottom on either side are incised a double ax and a scimitar
with sheath and sword-belt.

The date of the relief depends on that of the related arch at
Colonia Firma Julia Secundanorum Arausio, the modern Orange,
one of the most richly decorated arches in the Roman world

(north face, Fig. 4.6). The motifs are overwhelmingly military and naval. The oak leaves on the voussoirs of the side arches were the standard decoration of the civic crown, awarded to Ro-

4.6 Orange, arch

man soldiers who had saved a comrade's life in battle, and killed his opponent. The attic above these is crammed with trophies: bucklers, helmets, swords, spears, cloaks, Gallic trousers, harness, saddles, trumpets, battle-standards, and shields both decorated and inscribed. One of the motifs is the double Capricorn, the insignia of the Second Legion, which founded the colony in 36/5 B.C., and in A.D. 10 was allowed to take the name Augusta ("Augustus' Own"): Capricorn was his zodiacal sign. One of the inscriptions reads SACROVIR, the name of the Aeduan nobleman who in A.D. 21 led a revolt against high taxes, exorbitant interest rates, and brutal and arrogant Roman governors. Defeated in battle by the Second Legion, he committed suicide.

These details obviously have a bearing on the date of the arch. So does the interpretation of the put-holes for the bronze letters of the inscription which ran right across the fascia above the arches. As on the Maison Carrée in Nimes, the inscription appears to have had two phases. In the first, it honored the Second Legion; in the second, the Emperor Tiberius, according to whose twenty-eighth tribunate (A.D. 26, five years after Sacrovir's revolt) it is dated.

The frieze above the inscription is blank on the north side; on the other three it shows duels of Romans against naked, hairy barbarians, in which the Roman always wins.

The lateral reliefs above the frieze are remarkable. They represent the largest known collection of naval spoils: prows, ramming-beaks, figureheads, tridents, tillers, anchors, stern ornaments, masts, yardarms with ropes and pulleys, gangplanks. Since the Roman navy never fought a major engagement after the one with Antony and Cleopatra at Actium, this would seem to be the victory celebrated here. Julio-Claudian propaganda made it the symbol of Roman defeat of the barbarian.

Above the naval trophies are altar-like projections bearing on their face the instruments of sacrifice used in the founding of colonies like this one.

The decoration of the voussoirs of the central arch consists of grapes, pine cones, apples, acorns, ivy, and wheat-ears, as on Augustus' Altar of Peace in Rome. The pediment now contains only put-holes; these were for bronze appliqués (gilded to avoid staining the stone with verdigris): a head flanked by gilded horns of plenty. The put-holes on either side of the pediment were for gilt bronze Tritons.

Above the pediment is a wide base, which once supported a bronze representation of Tiberius in a four-horse chariot. The base bears a relief in which Roman cavalry and infantry fight half-naked, trousered Gauls; one tries to hold in his spilled guts with a huge hand. The Capricorn insignia occurs again on a shield. The whole effect, though carefully composed, is one of three-dimensional confusion, as on the Great Altar of Zeus at Pergamum in Asia Minor*: tumult, violence, disorder, and above all pathos, for these scenes of carnage were carved by Gallic artisans—the conquered—to the order of their Roman conquerors. Their impact had to be symbolic rather than particular, for they are fifty-six feet above the ground.

The east and west ends of the arch, not visible in the photograph, contain, exactly as at Carpentras and in the same style, reliefs of male and female prisoners chained to trees crowned with arms; the Triton and cornucopia motifs are repeated. The ends are thirty feet wide, to allow more space for decoration. The arch is sixty-three feet high and sixty-five feet across the front, a symmetrical plan: lines drawn from the tops of the outer plinths to the top center of the façade enclose an equilateral triangle. There are two sets of footings, corresponding to the two phases of the arch revealed by the inscription. The total effect is one in which Hellenistic realism is made to serve the propaganda of Roman power.

The arch at Orange was not a functional part of the city wall,

GSS, Fig. 7.6.

which passed fifty meters south of it, and had a perimeter of just over two miles, enclosing 173 acres. The most impressive surviving monument within the walls is the theater, of nearly the same size and date as the one at Arles. Its most remarkable feature is the 121-foot wall behind the stage (Fig. 4.7), as high as a ten-story building: Louis XIV called it "the handsomest wall in my realm." It is handsome even in its present state, stripped of its marble revetment. The columns at the right of the photograph show that in its original state it provided a three-level architectural backdrop. There were once seventy-six columns, a frieze of Amazons, centaurs, and a Perseus—characters from Greek tragedy—and niches for statues: a Venus, and, in the central niche, a statue of Augustus, twice life-size, as at La Turbie. The fragment at the Emperor's right foot is a kneeling, trousered

4.7   Orange, theater

figure, a Gaul throwing himself upon the emperor's mercy: propaganda for clemency, as in the trophies elsewhere.

Under Augustus' successors, propaganda did not always conform to fact. Sacrovir's rebellion is one example of Gallic reaction to real or fancied Roman cruelty. Another occurred in A.D. 68, the last year of the reign of the hated Nero, when the emperor's legate Vindex, descended from Aquitanian kings, led an abortive rebellion which was only one chapter in the tortured history of the "Four Emperors' Year." The ultimate victor, Vespasian, who reigned A.D. 69-79, dedicated himself to the restoration of the Augustan peace. A document of his methods was discovered at Orange after World War II. Excavation for the strongroom of a bank turned up some fragments of marble ready for the lime-kiln, as at St.-Bertrand-de-Comminges; ultimately they tipped the scales at 1,100 pounds. What was discovered was a cadaster or land-survey (Fig. 4.8), a marble map of the area around Orange, extending over thirty-five miles north of the city, and for twelve miles from the Rhône eastward, the line of the river and the surveyors' grid being picked out in red. An inscription of A.D. 77 at the top of the map, which was probably affixed to the wall of the basilica, declared that Vespasian had decreed the restitution by squatters of public land, assigned by Augustus to the original colonists, which had been illegally occupied for some years. The inscription records the frontage, the tax per running foot per year, the fine, the name of the occupant, and the name of his bondsman. Taxes in arrears were subject to 6 percent interest. It turned out that municipal officials had been among the squatters, occupying the land through proxies, or by using dummy names. Half the land was reassigned, tax-free, to the colonists; a third (the most mountainous and least fertile) to native Gauls; and a sixth was reserved as community property, for grazing. Some of the plateau or mountain land, which must have contained quarries, was assessed high. Some marshland was too, when it was near a market town. Town lots were four times as valuable

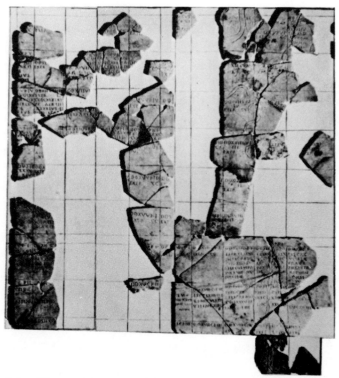

4.8   Orange, fragments of marble plan

as farmland. The whole document, designed to reduce Gallic discontent, is a fascinating example of the Roman legal mind at work: a nice eye for minutiae, and, on the whole, justice done; the Gauls gained something, and Roman citizens lost very little.

Measures like Vespasian's kept the Gauls happy and made them prosperous. The best archaeological evidence is the Pompeii of Provence, the little town of Vasio, nowadays Vaison-la-Romaine, a little over sixteen miles northeast of Orange. As with St.-Bertrand-de-Comminges, we owe our knowledge of and our pleasure in Vaison to the work of a dedicated amateur who made himself an expert, the Abbé (later Canon) J. Sautel. He first visited Vaison on a bicycle in 1907, and worked there steadily for nearly fifty years, until his death in 1955. The town was the capital of the Vocontii, who lived on the height south of the river Ouvèze (still spanned by a Roman bridge). About 20/19 B.C. they moved across the river onto more level ground, where the abbé excavated, and there they remained and prospered until the barbarians drove them up onto the height again, where one can now lunch charmingly at Le Beffroi in medieval surroundings.

The excavated area of Vaison (air photograph, Fig. 4.9) is divided into two quarters, Puymin, in the upper right quandrant, and La Villasse, in the center. In the lower left corner of the Puymin quarter Sautel excavated the House of the Messii (1), a luxurious residence with a pool surrounded by a peristyle, mosaic floors, frescoed walls, baths, and latrine. Sautel named it from a dedication he found in it to one Messia Alpina. On the evidence of the frescoes, the living quarters date from the first Christian century; the baths are a later addition.*

Adjoining the House of the Messii on the east is the Portico

---

*See *MSS* 220, paperback, 216. Frescoes are dated by their likeness to those at Pompeii, with an allowance for time-lag between Italy and the provinces. At Pompeii, the facts are:

STYLE	NAME	CHARACTERISTICS	DATE AT (POMPEII)
I	Incrustation	colored stucco, imitating marble	150-80 B.C.
II	Architectural	perspective; subjects from myth and religion	80 B.C.-A.D. 14
III	Egyptianizing	framed panels; miniaturist technique	A.D. 14-62
IV	Ornamental	infinite vistas; fantastic architecture	A.D. 62-79

of Pompey (Fig. 4.9, 2), so named from an inscribed fragment
of frieze found in it.. Pompey the Great had enfranchised many
Gauls. One of the most famous* was the universal historian Pompeius Trogus, who took his name in gratitude for achieving
Roman citizenship. The Pompeius after whom the Vaison portico
is named, the grandson of one of Pompey's beneficaries, was
himself a benefactor, a municipal officer and a priest of Rome
and Augustus in his native town. His gift to Vaison was a shaded,
watered garden (Fig. 4.10), now handsomely planted with roses.
It is 170 feet wide (its full length has not been excavated), with a
pool in the center which had in its walls fish-nests made of amphoras cut in two. To represent the statues which once adorned
it, Sautel placed in a niche a plaster cast of a marble copy of
Polyclitus' famous Diadoumenos, (boy binding his hair). The
marble copy, found in the 1860's, was sold to the British Museum. The portico's interior walls were originally stuccoed in
black, red, and green, in a style of the first Christian century;
coins range in date from Augustus to Diocletian, which means
that the portico was in use until the early fourth century of our
era.

Across the street to the east of the Portico of Pompey, the
abbé excavated several blocks of houses (Fig. 4.9, 3) much
more modest in size and décor than the House of the Messii.
North of them is a nymphaeum, or ornamental fountain-house (4),
with a tunnel adjoining on the west which led to the theater (5).

The theater is smaller than Arles', being 315 feet in diameter
as compared with 348. A remarkable number of statues and

---

*The most famous of all the sons of Vaison was not a Pompeius, but Sex.
Afranius Burrus, mentioned in an inscription as patron of the town,
who, jointly with the philosopher Seneca, was tutor to Nero during the
first five years of his reign, during which the young emperor is reported
to have behaved. Burrus died in A.D. 62.

4.9   Vaison-la-Romaine, air view

Puymin quarter
1. House of the Messii
2. Portico of Pompey
3. Residential quarter

4. Nymphaeum
5. Theater
6. Praetorium
M. Museum

La Villasse quarter

fragments, now in the site-museum (4.9, M), was found in its curtain slot. The subjects include Tiberius and members of his family; Hadrian, with a female variously identified as his wife Sabina or his mother-in-law Matidia; various municipal worthies in their best togas; Venus, Juno, Apollo, two statues of Bacchus, the patron of drama, and a miscellaneous assortment of hands, arms, feet, legs, and drapery. The statue of Tiberius has been used to date the theater in his reign and not later; the argument

4.10   Vaison-la-Romaine, Portico of Pompeius

being that he was so unpopular that statues of him would hardly have been put up *after* his reign. The year in which the practice of dedicating statues of Tiberius was most in fashion was A.D. 20/21.

The theater has been heavily restored (Fig. 4.11). The restoration provoked allegations of fraud: fake gouges in modern columns, artificial mutilations, ends of blocks deliberately hammered rough, to suggest ancient vandalism. Sautel rejoined that the

4.11   Vaison-la-Romaine, theater

restorations saved the theater from disintegrating, and that only ancient materials had been used in the rebuilding; he made no apology for the planting of shrubs and flower beds (see Fig. 4.9). The restoration may have been over-enthusiastic, but the result is charming to the lay eye, and annually brings thousands of visitors to Vaison who would not have crossed the street to see a site austerely left in a condition which only an archaeologist could love.

Southwest of the theater is the complex which Sautel christened the praetorium or military headquarters, though he thought the T-shaped building in the middle of the open space in the southern part of the complex might have been a temple of the Egyptian goddess Isis. Vast quantities of oyster shells suggest that the occupants, whether military or religious, had gourmet tastes. The colorful frescoes—yellow, red, and green—are in the first three Pompeian styles, and coins ranging from Augustus to Gordian III show that the building was in use at least until A.D. 244.

In the La Villasse quarter Sautel excavated one public building and a number of richly-decorated private houses. The public building was the commercial basilica (4.9, 7). The abbé re-erected the arch at its north end, and reported finding 300 fragments of polychrome marble paving. There were frescoes, with red panels bordered in yellow, and a green dado; and a latrine with seats for five. The building was in use until beyond the middle of the fourth century: the latest coins are of Constantius II, who died in A.D. 361. A main street (cardo: Fig. 4.9, 8, and Fig. 4.12) separated the basilica from the House of the Silver Bust. The photograph shows, on the right, a corner of the basilica, with shops set back to the north; on the left, the portico and shops which formed the east side of the House of the Silver Bust (4.9, 9). The bust after which the house is named is too corroded to reproduce. It is a homely bourgeois face, aptly compared by Sautel, in physiognomy and style, to the bust of Caecilius Jucundus found in Pom-

4.12   Vaison-la-Romaine, *cardo*

peii*, and therefore probably not much later than A.D. 79. The
prosperous proprietor expanded his holdings westward and swal-
lowed up the adjoining property, so that his mansion had two
peristyles, as well as the usual rather loud frescoes—red and
yellow panels, black and green borders. A charming find, reflect-
ing credit on the owner's taste, is an *oscilla*—a white marble disc

*MSS, Fig. 8.12.

designed to hang in the peristyle and swing in the wind—portraying in low relief a rabbit eating fruit from a basket. Sautel also
found a charming white marble appliqué of a sleeping child. The
latest coin is a small bronze of Valentinian I, who reigned from
A.D. 364 to 375.

South of the larger peristyle of the House of the Silver Bust,
and on a lower level, is the Atrium House (4.9, 10), with gay
frescoes in the "Developed First Style": in one room a dado with
yellow panels bordered in red; above it red panels with white
fillets and a black surround; elsewhere, a red or a black dado
with a surround of the opposite color; above, blue panels with
red surrounds. This house, like the basilica, lasted—on the evidence of coins—into the reign of Constantius II. North of the
large peristyle is the House of the Frescoes (4.9, 11), in the Third
Style, colorful as usual, the colors here including orange and pink,
with representations of animals: leopard, sea horse, deer, lion,
wild goat, a man with a doe, and a partridge in mosaic.

The House of the Dolphin (4.9, 12), excavated after World
War II, is named from a marble fragment found in it of a Cupid
riding a dolphin. It, too, has two peristyles and a mosaic floor.

The cathedral, west of La Villasse excavations (4.9, 13), has
an apse which dates from Merovingian times (sixth-seventh
Christian centuries), and shows what happened to Roman Vaison
after the barbarian invasions of the fourth century: the footings
(Fig. 4.13) are column-drums from the Roman city.

If it is easier in Vaison than on most Roman sites to imagine
the terraced levels of houses of the ancient town, the green gardens, the colonnades public and private lit by the warm light of
the Provençal sun, we owe it to the dedicated enthusiasm of the
Abbé Sautel. But Vaison was only one, and that not the most
important or prosperous, of the cities which flourished under
Roman rule in ancient Gaul. From one end of the province to
the other, "urban" connoted not blight, as today, but pleasant
living conditions and a true sense of community. This civilized

4.13   Vaison-la-Romaine, ancient column-drums
in cathedral footings

urbanity was the fruit of Romanization, and for it the Gauls
owed the Romans a great debt.

Western Aquitania, too, early enjoyed the benefits of Romanization. An excellent example is its early capital, Mediolanum
Santonum, now Saintes, where the evidence is an arch and an
amphitheater. The arch (Fig. 4.14) bears an inscription to Tiberius, his son Drusus, and his adopted son Germanicus. Since
Germanicus died in A.D. 19, the arch must be earlier than the date.
Its donor, named on the inscription, was a Romanized Gaul, the
same C. Julius Rufus whom we already met as the donor of the
Amphitheater of the Three Gauls at Lyon. The arch is much-
traveled. Rufus built it at the bridgehead on the east bank of the

4.14   Saintes, arch

Charente. By 1665, when we have a record of its repair, it had
been moved to the middle of the bridge. In the 1840s the bridge
was condemned as unsafe, and Prosper Mérimée, as inspector of
antiquities, moved in to save the arch. The mayor, proud of his
monument, but shaky in his Latin, proposed to rebuild it on a
nearby hillock. When Mérimée pointed out that the inscription

stated the arch was by the river, the worthy mayor proposed to change the inscription. Dishonors are equally shared here by Mérimée and the mayor. The inscription does mention a river or rivers; however, it is not the Charente but the confluence of the Rhône and Saône, the location of the Altar of the Three Gauls at Lyon, where the donor of the Saintes arch was a priest. Instead of throwing up his hands in despair, Mérimée arranged with the architect Clerget to have the arch dismantled stone by stone and set up again on its present site, which is roughly where it had been built in the first place.

The amphitheater (Fig. 4.15), on the western edge of the Roman city, is a little smaller than those of Arles and Nimes, about the same size (415 by 335 feet; arena, 210 by 128) as the one at Lyon, and used, between gladiatorial shows, for the same purpose, as a meeting place for the neighboring tribes. The evidence is an inscription, now lost, of Claudian date, perhaps A.D. 49, which

4.15   Saintes, amphitheater

bore the name of the Petrucorii, whose center was Périgueux, ninety miles southeast. Physically it most resembles the one at Fréjus. It had seventy-four arches, the gaunt remains of which stand out impressively in the photograph, and a colonnade at the top. It was built in a rocky valley, and the first two sections of seats (*maeniana*) are rock-cut. In it was found an altar with a relief showing a victorious athlete wearing a Gallic torque and proudly holding up his winnings, a purse of money.

The fruits of Romanization ripened early at Augustodunum, the present Autun. It will be recalled that this was the city settled in 12 or 7 B.C. at Augustus' direction by Aeduans brought down from their ancient stronghold at Bibracte. It prospered exceedingly, and became the intellectual center, as Lyon was the administrative, of Gaul. Its university was famous: to it the Gallic nobility sent its sons, of whom Sacrovir made hostages in the revolt of A.D. 21. Autun's walls were 3.6 miles in circumference, with fifty-four round towers; they enclosed 494 acres, as large an area as Arles or Nimes; the population may have been 80,000 (nowadays 18,500). They are said to have been mad about wine, as well they might, for the superb vineyards of Beaune and Nuits-St.-Georges, possibly in existence in the first Christian century, are less than thirty miles away. Two noble town gates survive, the Porte d'Arroux on the north and the Porte d'André on the east. The survival of the latter had an assist from the famous nineteenth-century restorer-architect Viollet-le-Duc. The gates have dual carriageways, with smaller arcades for the wall-walk above. They were originally flanked by round towers, making them resemble the Porta Nigra at Trier.*

Within the wall the university, of which unfortunately nothing remains, was at the very center of things, at the crossing of the cardo and the decumanus, with round temples in the Gallo-Roman fashion on either side of it.

*Romans on the Rhine, Fig. 8.3.

Autun had an amphitheater, larger than Arles' or Nimes'; this is where Sacrovir got the gladiators who fought for him. It also had a theater (Fig. 4.16), of which the photograph shows restoration in progress in the top two-thirds, with a view, at upper right corner, of the arches on which the top tier of seats rested. This theater was the largest in Gaul, with diameter of 485 feet and an alleged capacity of 33,000, and the fourth largest in the Empire; only those of Athens, Ephesus, and Smyrna exceeded it in size. A fragment of an inscription found in it during excavation by the unemployed in 1849 has been restored to read FLAVIO VESPASIANO; this would date it between A.D. 69 and 79. Another inscription mentions complete renovation, probably of the stage building, under Trajan, in A.D. 103. Coins show that it survived into the fourth century.

4.16   Autun, theater

Outside the city to the northeast rise starkly, to a height of seventy-seven feet, the brick-faced concrete walls, over seven feet thick, of the so-called Temple of Janus (Fig. 4.17). The put-holes under the upper relieving arches were for the sloping roof of a colonnade which surrounds it on all four sides, in the Gallo-Roman fashion. When it was new, in Nero's reign (on the evidence of a coin), it must have looked, on a larger scale (it is over fifty

4.17   Autun, "Temple of Janus"

feet square) like the north building in the temple precinct at Pesch.* Both buildings stood behind a precinct wall. Since the locality in which the temple stands is called Chaumar, a corruption of *Campus Martius*, it was probably dedicated to Mars, with a Gallic cult-title; the ascription to Janus has no scholarly authority. The latest coins show it to have been a casualty of a siege by the Gallic Emperor Tetricus in A.D. 270, which, even more tragically, destroyed the Burgundy vineyards. But they, and Autun itself, revived. Forty-one years later, when the Emperor Constantine visited it, the university was flourishing, and panegyrists saluted the city as the Athens of Gaul.

Vesunna Petrucoriorum, nowadays Périgueux, also boasts a Gallo-Roman precinct, this time with a round temple (Fig. 4.18), called the Tour de Vésone, dedicated to Vesunna, the patron goddess of the town. With its dimensions based on multiples of seven Roman feet—walls seven feet thick, width seven by eight, length with colonnade seven by fourteen—it has been called the most interesting building in Roman Gaul. It, too, has put-holes for the roof of a colonnade, and, higher up, windows which were later bricked up. The building was originally revetted with marble. The entrance was through a porch on the side with the gap, which according to local legend was made by St. Front with his crook. Its date is Hadrian's reign (A.D. 117-138), in Gaul as elsewhere in the empire a time of great architectural activity.

Prosperity continued through the second century, not always accompanied by good taste. The Porte Noire in Vesontio, now Besançon, is a case in point. Vesontio, in a spectacular setting in a loop of the River Doubs, was the capital of the Sequani. It had briefly been Julius Caesar's headquarters in 58 B.C., and about A.D. 167 was elevated to the rank of colony—*Colonia Victrix Sequanorum*—by the philosopher-emperor Marcus Aurelius, to

RoR, Fig. 6.12.

4.18   Périgueux, Tour de Vésone

commemorate a victory over the Germans. The Porte Noire, at the
south end of the cardo, was probably built at this time. The photograph (Fig. 4.19), taken under floodlights at night, shows how
ornate and over-decorated it is, like the arch at Orange, but there
the décor has a unifying symbolism, while here the motifs seem to
be taken at random from a pattern-book. Its columns—two stories
of them—intercolumniations, pilasters, voussoirs, attic, and passageway are all covered with reliefs, now much weathered, so
that there is controversy about the interpretation of some motifs.
The face of the voussoirs bears a Battle of Gods and Giants, by
now a cliché symbolizing Roman victory over barbarians. Victories fill the rest of the attic. In the passageway are battles, sieges,

and surrenders, which have some recognizable reference to Marcus Aurelius' German war. But the rest of the décor lapses into unimaginative riot. The pilasters, with six panels each, probably represent the months. The assortment on the columns and intercolumniations includes Mars (or Castor or Pollux); Hebe and Ganymede, the cupbearers to the gods; and a mythological

4.19   Besançon, Porte Noire

miscellany among which can be identified Minerva subduing a
giant, a Bacchic procession, Andromeda menaced by a sea mon-
ster, a couple of Labors of Hercules, Daedalus attaching the wings
of Icarus, Theseus with a Minotaur making an exceptionally silly
rhetorical gesture probably intended to represent a plea for mercy,
and two renditions of the mad Ajax slaughtering sheep which he
mistakes for human enemies. This is provincial art at its worst,
carved by a sculptor who does not understand his subject, under
the orders of a patron who cares less about meaning than about
spectacle. It is conspicuous consumption and conspicuous waste,
an example of the effect of too much money and too little taste.
Here the fruits of Romanization are clearly overripe.

Fruits are literally present in our final example, the reliefs of
the Porte de Mars (Fig. 4.20) in Durocortorum, nowadays Reims,
where the ceiling of the central vault shows, as at Besançon, the
agricultural activities appropriate to the months of the year, with
fruit-picking assigned to August. January to May do not survive,
but June is for horse-breeding, July for harvesting (with a mechanical reaper), September for hunting and plowing, October
for the vintage—this is champagne country—November for pas-
turing the flocks and pork-butchering, and December for bringing
the harvest home. In these unwarlike scenes the Romans have at
last, in these reliefs from the late second or early third Christian
century, broken away from the gloating representations of conquest which had disfigured the arches and trophies of the early
years of their occupation. (The seasons motif carried over into the
Middle Ages: seventy miles to the west, in the museum of Chan-
tilly, the finest example is preserved, the lovely miniatures in the
Book of Hours of the Duke of Berry, painted in 1410.) One of
the lateral vaults of the Porte de Mars bears a relief of the she-
wolf suckling Romulus and Remus. Romulus is the founder of
Rome, and Remus, according to local legend, is of course the

4.20   Reims, Porte de Mars

founder of the city of the Remi, Reims. The legend does more
credit to local patriotism than to historical or linguistic sense.

It is a pity that the other impressive Roman monument of
Reims is not open to the public. This is the second-century cryptoporticus under the Forum, in the Rue Colbert. Most visitors see
the cathedral, the champagne cellars, and perhaps the Porte de
Mars, and leave without even knowing the cryptoporticus is there.
Its massiveness is more impressive than any champagne cellar.
(It has been proposed that it be stocked with champagne and
opened as a tourist attraction.) It is U-shaped, 328 feet to a side,
with pier-supported double vaults 31 feet wide and 20 feet high,
and double-walled against dampness, for the structure served as a
granary, like those at Arles, Narbonne, and Bavai. It, too, can be
taken literally as an example of the fruitfulness which the Romans
brought to Gaul.

V

Country Houses and
Late-Empire Cities

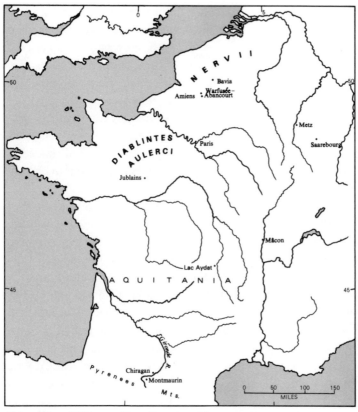

5.1 Map: Villas and late-Empire cities

127

It was not only in the cities that Rome changed the face of Gaul. The countryside, too, bore Rome's imprint, in the shape of hundreds of villas, some of which will be discussed in the first half of this chapter. A villa is a farmhouse. If it has a certain elegance, it is a *villa urbana*; if it is more useful than ornamental, it is a *villa rustica*. Gaul of course had farmhouses, as it had oppida, before the Romans. Rome's contributions were elegance, symmetry, and size. But even the most luxurious villae urbanae were the center of working farms. The Augustan architect Vitruvius, describing the ideal farmhouse, emphasizes its practical aspects, with only a passing word on elegance, though sumptuous villas abounded in his time. He stresses a healthy site, a southern exposure, the need for warmth in kitchen, cowhouses, baths, and oil-store, but for coolness in the wine cellar. He notes, and excavation has confirmed, that the main farmhouse is only a part of the estate: there should be separate sheep- and goat-folds, granary, stable, manger, barn, and bakehouse. He even comments on the need for good light, especially in corridors and stairwells, "because, in these, people carrying things often run into one another when they meet."

Some readers, associating Romans primarily with orgies, may be surprised at the Roman impact in Gaul on anything as literally down-to-earth as agriculture. But in fact the orgiasts were in a minority; otherwise the decline and fall would have happened centuries earlier than it did. In fact, agriculture was the cornerstone of Roman civilization, landholding was the qualification for citizenship, farming the most respected occupation. Rome was eager to set up in Gaul an establishment in her own image, and the discovery by archaeologists of hundreds of Gallo-Roman villas proves how eager the Gauls were to oblige. As long ago as 1906, 53 villas, 6 of them luxurious, were known in the neighborhood of Metz (see map, Fig. 5.1); by 1912, 99 had been found around Sarrebourg; by 1934, 150 were reported in the department of Yonne, and 30 more near Mâcon. Albert Grenier, in the same year, in a survey of villas all over France, commented on over 100, and published plans of 26. *Gallia*, the chief French journal of Roman archaeology, recorded 115 newly-discovered villae between 1945 and 1962. Three hundred seventeen were reported in 1961 in eleven cantons of the department of Corrèze, and since then air photography has revealed many more. In the single department of the Somme, around Amiens, 300 "rural establishments" have been identified from the air, 20 of them luxury villas. Fig. 5.2 shows one example, at Warfusée-Abancourt, a dozen miles east of Amiens. In 1968, air photographers using a red filter identified 12 villas in the plain of Aix.

Of course the agricultural exploitation of Gaul was not without its problems, involving large estates, absentee landlords, sharecroppers, and, eventually, tenant farmers bound to the land like serfs on a medieval manor. But there was a sunny side to the picture, too. The Christian Tertullian, certainly no friend to the Roman establishment, could write, about A.D. 210, "Flourishing farms have cancelled out the desert [Tertullian was an African],

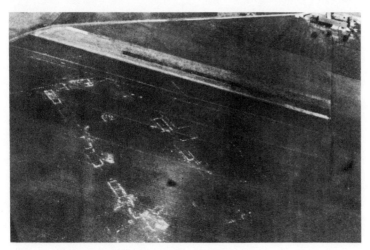

5.2   Warfusée-Abancourt, villa, air view

tilled fields have tamed the forests, flocks and herds have put wild beasts to flight. Sandy places are seeded, rocky places planted, marshes drained . . . Everywhere houses, people, law and order, civilized life." Salvian, writing in A.D. 440, when much of Gaul had been overrun by barbarians, can still speak of Aquitania's well-watered, fertile beauty, with its vineyards, meadows, plowland, orchards, fields of waving grain—in short, an earthly paradise.

Literature illuminates archaeology particularly well in a verse letter describing his villa, written by Sidonius Apollinaris to a friend between A.D. 460 and 465. Sidonius, son-in-law of an emperor, prefect of Rome, and later a bishop, had his villa on Lac Aydat, about six miles southwest of Gergovia, where the Gauls had worsted Caesar over 500 years before. Most, if not all, of what Sidonius describes can be matched in the excavated villas. His house, which he modestly describes as a "cabin" or "hut," enjoys a view of mountain, hill, and lake. The baths are convenient to the forest, which supplies wood for their furnace. There is an indoor pool as big as those in public baths, with seats around it, and a vaulted roof lit by clerestory windows. Its walls are of local stone, stuccoed white, and Sidonius emphasizes, as befits a future bishop, that there are no pornographic pictures of actors or athletes, only chaste verses in modest praise of the architecture. From the covered pool a triple passage leads to the outdoor pool, over 200 square yards of it, fed—we gather somewhat noisily— by six lifelike lion's head spouts. The women's quarters adjoin. A portico, with modest columns of brick, overlooks the lake. There is a covered walkway to a summerhouse, and a winter dining room. In a smaller dining room Sidonius and his friends can sit at a round table, with a view of the lawn and lake, and drink snow-cooled wine while they watch men fishing with cork floats on their lines. The poet's list of sleep-inducing rural noises seems better calculated to produce insomnia: it includes locusts, frogs, swans, geese, roosters, crows, nightingales, swallows, shepherds' pipes, cowbells, and the lowing of cattle. There is a grove nearby where, after this somewhat cacophonous siesta, host and guest could toss a ball about under the lime trees. Such luxury, with the barbarian prowling at the gates, may be taken as a symptom of decline and fall. It is also testimony to Rome's civilizing influence in Gaul.

Many of the features Sidonius mentions with modest pride supply the clues which the modern archaeologist uses to identify a villa site: baths, pools, porticoes, marble paving or revetments. There are often other clues, which in his modesty Sidonius does not mention, especially mosaics, statuary, and frescoes. All of these appear in one of the most famous of Gallic luxury villas, at Chiragan, near Martres-Tolosanes, less than thirty miles downriver toward Toulouse from St.-Bertrand-de-Comminges. It is the second largest villa known outside Italy. Its enclosure wall (ABCFG on the plan, Fig. 5.3) is nearly a mile around, surrounding a tract of forty acres, an area as large as Cosa, a Latin colony in Italy built for 2,500 families. The villa itself covered seven and a half acres.

The excavator was able to distinguish four building phases, the first and simplest of which he identified as Augustan, on the evidence of a coin of Augustus' right-hand man Agrippa. In this first phase the villa consisted of rooms grouped around a peristyle (see the plan).

To the second period—Trajanic, A.D. 98–117—belongs the southern extension, by means of a court bordered by cryptoporticoes, to a summerhouse (like Sidonius'; at F) overlooking the Garonne river. The cryptoportico east of the peristyle and a new and more luxurious bath-block also belong to this period.

The third period—Antonine and Severan, roughly the last half of the second Christian century—saw the heyday of the villa. The construction was in Pyrenees marble, from the quarries of St.-Béat. The fountain court, and two miniature "dower houses," one

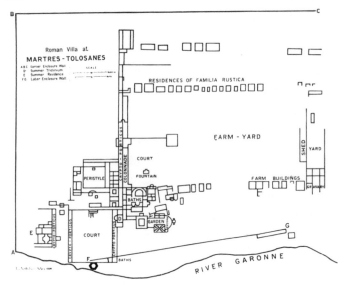

5.3   Chiragen, villa, plain

east of the baths, the other west of the Trajanic court, were built
then. South and southeast of the baths a whole new complex was
added: from west to east it included an apsidal summer dining
room (again like Sidonius'), with a passage leading to an atrium,
and an enclosed garden ending in a curvilinear recess with seats,
called an exedra; and another summerhouse, like the one overlooking the river. To this period belongs a whole series of statues, found west of the Trajanic court, where they were dumped
by barbarians or Christians in the fifth century of our era. Since
they portray emperors from Augustus to Septimius Severus, they
have given rise to the hypothesis that the villa belonged to an imperial official, but the owner may have been simply a particularly
loyal landed proprietor of unusual wealth. A broken inscription
on a broken bust may bear his name, Aconius Taurus. The most
charming find was not the routine bust of an emperor, but the

delightful head of a curly-headed baby, in Greek marble, (Fig. 5.4), now in the Musée St.-Raymond, in Toulouse.

The final period—the fourth Christian century—saw the concentration at the villa of all the practical activities of the estate. The archaeological evidence for this is the set of buildings, in four rows, running east and west from the north Trajanic cryptoportico. The northernmost row is a series of stalls: the ex-

5.4 Chiragan, marble head of baby

cavator calculated they would have held thirty yoke of oxen. The second file, of twenty sturdy tile-roofed buildings, contained quarters for about a hundred farm families; their tools and household implements—chisels, whetstone, hand-mill—were found in the houses. The third row, an extension eastward of the Antonine "dower house," contained eleven workshops, in which so many loomweights were found that the assumption is that all the weaving for the estate was done there.

The second and third rows of buildings were connected, at their east end, by a perpendicular group enclosing a farmyard. This group contained barns and sheds for the storing of hay and grain, built around three sides of a yard. A good deal of ingenuity has gone into calculating, from the capacity of the barns, the probable acreage of the estate and the number of hands it supported. The capacity of the barns is 11,350 bushels. The modern yield is 28 bushels per acre. If we assume half that yield in antiquity (on account of shallow plowing and inadequate fertilizer), we find that to produce this amount of grain would require 800 acres of land. But the proprietor's share was only a third; therefore the total acreage of the estate was probably 2,400, or more, if the crops were rotated. At an average of one workman per 6.6 acres, for which we have ancient authority, this gives a total working population of 363; at four to a family, they could just be housed in the living quarters described above. We do not know how they got on with the lord of the manor, but whatever the relations, they must have been looked back on with nostalgia by the survivors of the fire which accompanied the Vandal invasion of 408. The date is derived from coins of Arcadius, who reigned from A.D. 395 to 408. Chiragan was not as lucky as Sidonius' villa: its sculpture was broken, its handsome buildings reduced to heaps of rubble, or its stones robbed to build the village of Martres-Tolosanes three-quarters of a mile to the north.

The largest, best-excavated, and best-publicized luxury villa in all France is at Montmaurin, twenty miles west of Chiragan, and

twelve miles north of St.-Bertrand-de-Comminges, in a countryside rich in wheat fields, vineyards, and stands of timber—oak,
chestnut, ilex, elm, maple—convenient to quarries and clay-pits
for stone, brick, and tile. Over the years the villa has been subject to every form of depredation, some unusual: its columns
were used as rollers in the fields, its marbled and frescoed walls
ruined by pigeon-hunters, a mosaic uprooted because legend
said a golden goat lay under it. (It didn't.) However, since 1947
the villa has been carefully excavated (2,000 cubic meters of
earth moved), with the full cooperation of the present owner of
the land, but not without hazard; the director of excavations,
Georges Fouet, reports the killing of eighteen vipers per half-day's
work, for a total bag of 650.

The results have been astonishing: a palace of nearly 200
rooms, planned with axial symmetry and decorated with restrained taste (see air view, Fig. 5.5); the villa covering ten acres;
the estate, with twenty-two farm buildings, 3,750. Chiragan
seems small by comparison.

The villa in its latest phase dates, on the evidence of coins,
from about A.D. 350. It succeeded a building a century older,
which was destroyed by barbarians in about 276; before that, it
had been a villa rustica, dating from about A.D. 50.

The entrance was through a D-shaped portico, 175 feet wide
and 70 deep, called by Fouet the Court of Honor. It had a semicircular colonnade in which the width of the walkway matched
the distance between the columns. The hexagonal structure in
the left half of the D is a Gallic shrine enclosing an altar. Coins
left by the pious as offerings are most numerous from Constantine's reign (A.D. 312–337), and cease after 388. A layer of greasy
black earth beside the altar is what remains of the offerings of
first-fruits; dogs were also sacrificed. Though one of several other
altars is inscribed to Jupiter, he will have been a Gallic deity,
called by a Roman name out of courtesy: this is a Gallic shrine,
which probably existed before the latest phase of the villa. The
D-shaped portico was planned to respect the shrine, and its lo-

5.5   Montmaurin, villa, air view

cation made it possible for peasants to pay their respects there without entering the villa.

For those who did want to enter, waiting-rooms were provided in the antechambers north of the Court of Honor: that for the gentry was hypocaust-heated, that for the peasants not. These waiting-rooms form the south side of a vast peristyle measuring 6,458 square feet. The other wings contained the cool summer and the heated winter dining rooms, the kitchen, and other rooms whose precise function is not known. The rooms glowed with color, even gold being included in the wall mosaics. The assigned date is A.D. 325.

North of the large peristyle is another one, apsidal, with a summerhouse at the back. The hollow receptacles in the walls are tanks in which fish for the table could be kept alive until wanted. The owners of the villa were gourmets; Fouet found twenty-two different kinds of shellfish, as well as snails and the appropriate implement to eat them with. There were garden plots in the apses, and the walls were painted, or veneered with matched marble sawn from the same block and applied so that the veins fitted, as in marquetry work. The painted walls either imitated marble—in the so-called "fried egg" technique—or represented vegetation or landscape.

The apsidal complex at the left center of the photograph is the baths. Fig. 5.6 gives a detail, showing the marble pavement, and re-erected columns in the green-veined marble called cipollino, with plain Tuscan capitals. Restraint in décor is a welcome characteristic of Montmaurin. The model (Fig. 5.7), made at a later stage in the excavations than the air photographs, shows, to the left of the baths, the working part of the villa, with stables, a forge, and farmhands' quarters arranged around a farmyard. Finds of sheep shears, chisels, a plumb-bob, a gouge, hobnails, and veterinarians' instruments, including one for castrating animals, show the sort of work that was done, and suggest that the villa was intended to be self-sufficient. Some of the dishes were of wood

5.6   Montmaurin, villa, nymphaeum

instead of pottery, as is still the case in Gascony. Fouet reports
550 pottery mortars, but no pestles; these must have been made
of wood. Pets included a cat and a kitten: Fouet found their paw-

5.7   Montmaurin, villa, model

marks, made in wet tile. A dice box and game counters show how the owner and his guests might use their leisure time, though they might also have gone riding, walking, hunting, or fishing.

Among the more valuable finds were imported *millefiori* glass, multicolored and striated, and statues or heads of Adonis, the Egyptian god Serapis, and Venus. A local farmer has set up, discreetly veiled by shrubbery, one of his finds, a twenty-inch phallus; which the village abbé, in his innocence, had failed to recognize for what it was. A villa of this size naturally yielded an immense amount of pottery; including 1,550 vases of a "good" period (A.D. 50-150), most of it local ware; 3,000 later pieces, imported from Spain. Montmaurin was at an important crossroads of the north-south route over the Pyrenees to Spain and the east-west route which connects the Mediterranean with the Atlantic. This location brought it prosperity, but also a tragic end.

It was in the path of the Vandals on their marauding way to Spain in the early fifth century of our era; they set it on fire, and it was never rebuilt.

Montmaurin and Chiragan will suffice as examples of great luxury villas, since they are representative of the general style. But it is important to remember that the villas were significant because of their number, their impact upon the Gallic economy, and their foreshadowing of the medieval manorial system. As towns declined in the late Empire, refugees from them put themselves under the protection of the lords of manors like Montmaurin, which were like tiny kingdoms and represented a new form of colonization.

We turn next to an example of a town in decline. Bagacum, nowadays Bavai, was an important road-center, the capital of the Nervii, a Belgic tribe which gave Julius Caesar a great deal of trouble. Its road connections were with the English Channel at Gesoriacum (Boulogne); via Reims with the capital of the Three Gauls at Lyon; and with the Rhine at Cologne. A charming local legend connects the building of this latter road with the redoubtable Valkyrie Brünnhilde. Like Reims, Bavai had a vast cryptoporticus (Fig 5.8), measuring 820 by 328 feet, with a double-vaulted gallery 32 feet wide and 15 feet high. As elsewhere, the walls were double, against damp, so that this, too, may have been a warehouse, under the Forum, though it is finished with unusual care for so mundane a use, and the means of access so far discovered—a single stair near the north corner—seem inadequate. Abutting on the outer walls of the gallery were shops, those on the west side opening on the decumanus. A substructure measuring 100 by 230 feet, in the middle of the open area, must be the foundations of a temple of impressive size, probably the Capitolium. The photograph looks northwest, across the nave and aisles of the basilica. The rubble core visible above and behind the basilica is what remains of a late rampart wall:

5.8   Bavai, cryptoporticus

this is the evidence for decline. Coins date the cryptoporticus to the flourishing age of the Antonines, the mid-second century of our era. Sometime between 257 and 276 Bavai was sacked; it recovered as a tiny stronghold, built by incorporating the remains of the fallen vaults of the cryptoporticus into a rampart wall with half-round towers, constructed against the perimeter walls of the cryptoporticus. Thus the protected area of a once-prosperous town was compressed into a space of about six acres. The same thing happened all over Gaul, from the last half of the third

century onward. Once-extensive cities like Autun, Nimes, Périgueux and many others reduced their walled areas to a mere
fraction of their former size. As the cities dwindled, the villa
population grew. When the villas in their turn were overrun by
the barbarians, the survivors stole the stone from the ruined villas
to build nearby—as Martres-Tolosanes was built from the ruins
of Chiragan—the villages which are the characteristic unit of
medieval France: "village" is obviously derived from "villa."

However unimportant Paris may have been in antiquity, its
pride of place in modern France justifies our taking it as an example of a Gallo-Roman town of the later Empire. We saw that
when Labienus attacked it, its center was on the Ile de la Cité.
A burnt level under the present Marché aux Fleurs testifies to the
Gallic scorched-earth policy against Labienus. There was apparently a Roman headquarters building under the Palais de Justice;
its date is uncertain. The remains visible in the summer of 1969
under the Place du Parvis Notre-Dame included part of a rampart
from the third century after Christ, and a couple of hypocaust-
heated rooms. On the whole the island seems in the high empire to
have been subordinate in importance to the Left Bank.

The Latin Quarter was the center of Roman Paris (see plan,
Fig. 5.9). The Rue St.-Jacques was the cardo, the river was the
decumanus. The Forum lay under the present Rue Soufflot, between the Rue St.-Jacques and the Boulevard St.-Michel. It
measured 525 by 328 feet, and was surrounded by a portico with
shops. At its west end was a temple facing east, probably dedicated to Rome and Augustus. A basilica closed its east end. Very
much the same plan is to be seen at St.-Bertrand-de-Comminges,
Alésia, and Augst.* By the time of Trajan this kind of Forum
arrangement had become canonical in city-planning; the central
authority imposed the formula, at Paris as elsewhere.

*RoR, Figs. 2.6 & 7.

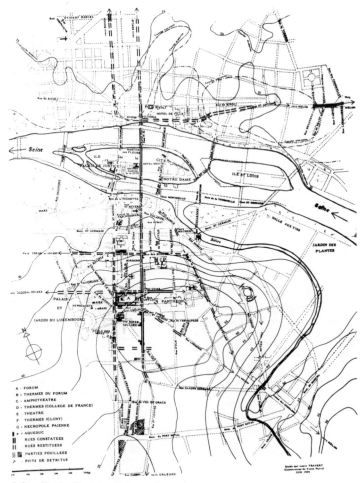

A · FORUM
B · THERMES DU FORUM
C · AMPHITHEATRE
D · THERMES (COLLEGE DE FRANCE)
E · THEATRE
F · THERMES (CLUNY)
G · NECROPOLE PAIENNE
▌ ● · AQUEDUC
▌▌ RUES CONSTATEES
▌▌ RUES RESTITUEES
▓ ▓ PARTIES FOUILLEES
⌐ · PUITS DE DETRITUS

5.9   Paris, Roman town, plan

Paris had three sets of public baths. The smallest and oldest, dating from about mid-first century of our era, lie under the Rue Gay-Lussac, opposite the Gare du Luxembourg. Another set was found in 1935, in digging the foundations of a new east wing for the Collège de France. A round pool, heated by an ingenious combination of hypocaust and conduit, has parallels at Hadrian's Villa near Tivoli in Italy, at Fontaines-Salées, to be discussed in the next chapter, and at Calleva, modern Silchester, in Hampshire. These baths belong to the high Empire, to the Antonine or Severan dynasties (*ca.* A.D. 175-225).

But the most interesting and best-preserved set of Parisian baths is incorporated in the fabric of the Hôtel de Cluny, at the corner of the Boulevard St.-Germain and the Boulevard St.-Michel (Fig. 5.10). More was discovered about the plan of these baths when an air-raid shelter was dug in the grounds of the Hôtel early in World War II, and work was continued for ten years after the war. What emerged was the plan of a complex from the second or third Christian century, of sixteen or seventeen rooms, covering an area of 328 by 213 feet. The most interesting part of the baths is the *frigidarium* or cold-plunge room (70 by 40

5.10   Paris, Cluny baths

feet), which, as the archaeologist in charge, Professor P.-M. Duval, points out with pardonable pride, is the only large Roman hall in the West which has its walls and vaults intact. They stand 50 feet high to the top of the vault, and owe their excellent state of preservation to their having been used in the eighteenth century as a cooper's workshop and storeroom. The ribs of the vaults rest on consoles in the shape of ships' prows, one of which is visible in the upper left quadrant of the photograph. Reliefs of fish, helmets, shields, cuirasses, javelins, and greaves embellish the consoles. Duval thinks these are the symbols of the local guild of boatmen, the *nautae Parisiaci*, who transported supplies for the Roman army, and may have donated the baths and used the appropriate rooms in them for guild meetings. A dedication of theirs, found in re-use under the choir of Nôtre-Dame, is on display on a pedestal under the central window (see photograph); it will be discussed in more detail in the next chapter. The tradition of these boatmen lived long: there is a ship on the coat of arms of Paris, which every gendarme wears on his breast. It bears an appropriate motto: FLUCTUAT NEC MERGITUR, "It rocks, but it does not sink."

The baths were fed by an aqueduct with its source at Rungis, ten miles south of Paris. Arceuil, halfway along its course, is famous in French literature as the site of a gay end-of-term picnic held there in July 1549, which the prince of poets of his time, Pierre de Ronsard, described in lyric and classical detail. The aqueduct had a capacity of 2,000 cubic meters a day, enough to supply the needs of a population of 4,600. The importance of Paris did not really begin until its duke, Hugh Capet, made it the capital of his kingdom in A.D. 987.

The other major Roman building in Paris is the amphitheater in the Rue Monge (Fig. 5.11). Its arena measures 172 by 153 feet, which would make its overall dimensions about the same as those of the amphitheater at Nimes, four or five times too big for the local population. The shows must have attracted spectators from miles around. The attraction was double, for the building,

5.11   Paris, amphitheater

like the one at Augst,* was also used as a theater. The reconstructed footings in the foreground of the photograph are those
of a stage building surrounded by seats in an ellipse on three sides.
The stage could be used for dance, mime, and declamation, the
arena for gladiatorial shows and beast-fights. Duval dates it in the
first Christian century; it was destroyed in a barbarian raid in the
beginning of the third. Nowadays it is used on summer evenings
for outdoor performances of such plays as *The Barber of Seville*
or *The Taming of the Shrew*.

RoR, Fig. 2.8.

Paris also had a small conventional theater, under the Rue Racine and the Lycée St.-Louis. It was smaller than the Odeon at Lyon, which held 3,000. If there was a circus or a hippodrome, it probably lay under the site of the Halles aux Vins, now the scientific center of the university; no remains have been discovered, to my knowledge.

On the right bank, a temple to Mercury lies under the church of St. Pierre, on Montmartre, whose name means Mt. Mercury. Four columns from the Roman temple are visible in re-use in the church.

Forum, baths, and amphitheater make of Roman Paris a most respectable example of Romanization for so small a town. One would have to multiply this example many times in order to appreciate the full extent of the Romanization of Gaul in the prosperous Antonine period. But after about A.D. 250 the Parisians returned to the insular life they had known three centuries before, in the days of Labienus' attack upon the Gallic oppidum. And so we look for the administrative center of medieval Paris on the Ile de la Cité. But there is something appropriately symbolic in the fact that the intellectual center, the Quartier *Latin*, grew up on the site the Romans had chosen as the seat of the *urbanitas* and the *humanitas* which was their most precious gift to their provinces.

What made the urbanity and the humanity of Roman Gaul possible was the easy passage of goods and ideas. They traveled by the road network which Agrippa had begun and successive emperors had continued, facilitating fast communication between villa and town, between city and city, with the whole net centering in Lyon. The main highways were imperial post roads, where messengers on official business could find fresh relays of horses at *mutationes* spaced ten or twelve Roman miles apart, with larger stations, called *mansiones*, supplying overnight accommodations at intervals of twenty or more miles. As the barbarians became

more menacing, a system of road police grew up, with stations at
fortified *castella*, which also contained warehouses for storing the
proceeds of taxes paid in kind.

One of the best-preserved of these fortified castella is near
Noviodunum, nowadays Jublains (see Fig. 5.12), on the main
Roman road from Lyon to Brittany. Its core is a 108 by 74-foot
structure built round an atrium, with square corner towers, store-
rooms, and baths. Its walls are nearly 7 feet thick. But they in
turn are protected by two other ramparts, one of earth, the other
of stone. The earthwork measures 213 by 246 feet and is 32 feet
thick. The outer masonry wall's dimensions are 413 by 377 feet;
it is over 15 feet thick and is protected by towers. It is built of
granite, and still stands 13 to 16 feet high in places. The fill between the faces of the wall contains architectural members and
sculpture which must be the debris from a barbarian sack of the

5.12   Jublains, fortified Roman way-station

nearby town, probably in A.D. 256. (The town was the capital of the Aulerci Diablintes, and contained a temple, baths, and a theater.) The last and most numerous coins—110 pieces—are of Tetricus, A.D. 270-274. The total life-span of the castellum was less than twenty years, from one invasion to another. Jublains, insignificant as it is in itself, is a short-lived example of that infinite capacity for taking pains which kept the empire together for 300 years and more. Efficiency is part of the explanation; tolerance is another. Roman tolerance of the religion of the empire's subjects will be the subject of the next chapter.

VI

Shrines and Statues

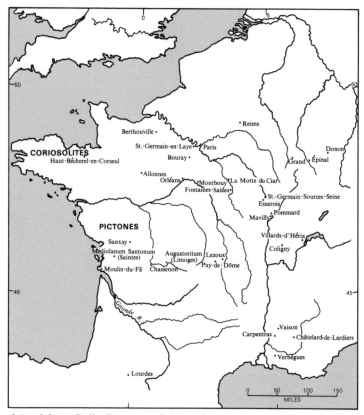

6.1   Map: Gallo-Roman religious sites

Happy is the nation that has no history. Thanks to the Romans, Gaul prospered generally for 300 years after Caesar's conquest. The Gallic peace, which allowed cities to prosper and villas to flourish, was due in large part to Roman tolerance of Gallic religious beliefs. So long as the Gauls paid lip service to Roman official religion, emperor-worship, the Romans allowed them to worship their own gods in their own way. This chapter describes nineteen places revealed by archaeology where this tolerance prevailed. Nine of these appear in no guidebook and would be worth a pilgrimage, mercifully away from the beaten track. Such a tour would combine a study of Gallo-Roman remains with other pleasures: magnificent views, winter sports, the enjoyment of beach resorts; Romanesque, Gothic and modern architecture and history; and, last but not least, gastronomy.

The Romans tolerantly turned a blind eye to the Gauls' observance of their own religion so long as the provincials paid their taxes and behaved. This indulgence was helped by the Roman practice of identifying Gallic gods with their own, which they thought they could recognize in Gallic disguises, including Mercury, Apollo, Mars, Jupiter, and Vulcan.

The shrines and statues to be discussed in this chapter are scattered over most of France, the northeast and southwest excepted (see map, Fig. 6.1). Three of them are within easy reach of Paris: Berthouville and Bouray, where Mercury was worshiped, and Allonnes, the site of a shrine of Mars. A visit to the first two will take the tourist out of the feverish hurry of modern Paris into the bourgeois tranquillity of its near environs. Allonnes, on the other hand, adjoins Le Mans, which every June is the most feverish place in Europe, thanks to the international auto races.

A visit to another set of shrines could be combined with the pleasures of Burgundian food and wine, as well as with the nearby Caesarian site of Alesia. These are Mavilly, which may be Druid; La Motte du Ciar, sacred to Vulcan, which lies just

south of Sens, where the Hôtel de Paris et de la Poste is justly fa-·
mous for its snails, chicken, duck, and Chablis; and St.-Germain-
Sources-Seine and Fontaines Salées, healing springs in the very
heart of the Burgundy wine country. The latter lie in the valley below the famous twelfth-century church of Vézelay, where Bernard
of Clairvaux preached the Second Crusade, and Richard the Lion-
Hearted, before the Third, met with Philip-Augustus of France
to plan the release of Jerusalem from Saladin.

East of the Burgundian pagan holy places are three hilltop
sanctuaries where Gallo-Roman studies might in season be pleasantly blended with winter sports: the Mercury shrine at Donon,
that of Mars at Villards d'Héria, and Apollo's sacred place at
Grand; the last is conveniently close to the birthplace of the national saint and heroine, Joan of Arc.

Two sites in the southeast have other than religious attractions:
Mercury's at Châtelard-de-Lardiers offers both winter sports and
delicious cheese; Jupiter's at Vernègues is on the route between
Aix and Arles; nearby are the lofty romantic ruins of Les Baux
(after which the mineral bauxite is named); in the Middle Ages
troubadours sang there, and below the ruined town, at La Bau-
manière, the gourmet may now enjoy one of the finest meals to
be had in France, washed down with the wines of Gigondas or
Tavel.

Mercury's shrines in central France are Lezoux and Puy-de-
Dôme; the former is also the site of famous ancient potteries; the
latter affords one of the finest panoramic views in France; at both,
the traveler may enjoy a balloon glass of Armagnac, which con-
noisseurs prefer to any other brandy.

Argenton, which adjoins a possible Druid site in central
France, is itself a town worth seeing, with picturesque balconied
houses bordering the main street. In west-central France, there
are Apollo's shrine at Sanxay, the sacred springs of Chassenon,
and Mars' tower at Moulin-du-Fâ. This is pleasant dairyland,
noted for its cheese, and pleasantly free of tourists. Near Moulin-

du-Fâ is Royan, whose church of Notre Dame is one of the landmarks of the New Architecture in Europe; also nearby is one of
the country's finest beaches.

Finally, one may visit the Mars sanctuary at Bécherel in Brittany together with the standing stones of Carnac and finish the
day, in the proper season, with a feast of succulent oysters. Such
are the fringe benefits which the pious pilgrim to the pagan
shrines of France can derive. We now turn to a discussion of the
sites themselves.

"The Gauls," says Caesar, "are completely addicted to religious observance." Archaeology bears him out. Sanctuaries,
statues, reliefs, and statuettes of Gallic gods abound, and they
show a refreshing independence of Roman religious conventions.
The Romans knew the value of religion as an opiate for the common people. A naturally superstitious race like the Gauls, given
free rein to worship their own gods in their own way, would, the
Romans thought, hanker less after political independence.

Caesar's account of Gallic religion in his *Commentaries* is
brief but famous. He began with the Druids, whom he described
as a powerful priestly caste under an arch-Druid, supervising
sacrifices, acting as judges with powers of excommunication, pre-
siding over an annual assembly at a holy place in central Gaul—
probably near Orléans (see map, Fig. 6.1),* though there is no
archaeological evidence—and exempt from taxes and military
service. Therefore, says Caesar drily, students and postulants
flock to them for long training in astronomy, physics, and theo-
logy. As an example of Gallic superstition, Caesar cited human

---

*Controversial claims are made for another site in central Gaul as Druid.
This is St. Marcel (Indre), near Argenton, the ancient Argentomagus.
Here excavation has revealed a theater (Augustan to Flavian), an amphitheater, baths, a Roman bridge, a rich necropolis, and, possibly, a monumental fountain served by a vaulted drain tall enough for a man to stand
upright.

sacrifice: the burning of criminals in wickerwork cages. In an attempt to make Gallic gods meaningful to Roman readers, Caesar identified them, not always legitimately, with alleged Roman equivalents. Thus he called their principal god Mercury, whose statues, he said, are numerous up and down Gaul, as indeed archaeologists have found them to be; Mercury is the patron of the arts and trade, and a guide to travelers. The Gauls, Caesar continued, also worship Apollo, god of healing. Mars, god of war, Jupiter, their sky-god, and Minerva, patroness of crafts. They believe themselves descended from Dispater, god of the underworld, and therefore reckon time by nights rather than days.* They celebrate festivals on the first of the month. Their funerals are rich and expensive: treasures are burned on the pyre, and, not long before Caesar's time, favorite slaves and retainers were immolated as well.

Much of this is superficial and confused, derived from Greek authors who themselves had no first-hand knowledge of Gallic religion. The archaeological evidence, though often puzzling and equivocal, usually gives a better idea than Caesar does of the fascinating ways in which Gallic religious beliefs and practices differed from the Roman.

One wishes that archaeologists had found a representation of a white-robed Druid climbing an oak tree to cut mistletoe with a golden sickle, as Pliny the Elder tells us they used to do. But no such representation exists, nor has any Druid sanctuary, recognizable as such, been found. The Druid gods dwelt in temples not made with hands. The nearest thing to a monument with Druid associations—and even this is controversial—is the pillar of Mavilly. It is now in Beaune; and there is a cast in the museum of St.-Germain-en-Laye. Each face of the pillar bears two reliefs, described by one scholar as eligible for first prize in an ugliness

---

*The calendar of Coligny, inscribed on stone, proves Caesar right on this point.

contest, but we are interested in them as documentation, not as art. They portray, in Roman terms, (1) Jupiter seated, with eagle and scepter; (2) Neptune, with dolphin and staff, and wearing a Gallic torque; (3) the smith-god Vulcan and the hearth-goddess Vesta; (4) Mars, Minerva, and a ram-headed serpent. Mars wears the torque and a coat of mail. He carries a lance and a hexagonal shield, like those on the arch at Orange; this dates the reliefs in the reign of Tiberius. The fifth relief is of a female figure holding a horn of plenty, and attended by a diminutive male; the pair have been identified as the Mother-Goddess and her consort: in Graeco-Roman mythological terms, Cybele and Attis. The sixth relief is of a female figure, against a background of leaves and flowers. She carries a torch, and is accompanied by two serpents. Perhaps she is Hygieia, goddess of health, or the river goddess Sequana (the healing springs of the source of the Seine are only thirty-five miles to the north of Mavilly). The seventh figure is naked and winged, like the Roman Mercury; his attributes, however are those of Roman Hercules, a lion and a club. The eighth relief is the most controversial, and the one which may be interpreted as representing a Druid: the figure in the foreground (Fig. 6.2), holding what may be a box of eye-salve, for treatment of the figure standing behind, with his hands to his eyes. (Along with their other accomplishments. Druids were held capable of making more or less miraculous cures.) The bird in the relief would then be an eagle, the sharpness of whose vision was proverbial, and the dog is a familiar figure in healing cults: at Greek Epidaurus the lick of a sacred dog cured blindness.* The aim of the dedicator will have been to collect as many gods as possible, in order to improve his chances of a cure. The findspot of the pillar is near healing springs, and some of the gods portrayed have associations with water: Neptune, for example, is the god of fresh water as well as salt. The connection with Druids

*See *GSS*, 280; paperback, 262-263.

6.2 Mavilly pillar, healing of eye disease, relief

is tenuous, but that with healing springs is plausible. We shall
have occasion later on to cite other examples of hydrotherapeutic
sanctuaries.

Following the order in which Caesar names the Gallic gods, we proceed to Mercury. The Romans equated him with the Greek Hermes, who made the first lyre out of a tortoise shell, conducted the souls of the dead to Hades, and protected merchants and wayfarers. His attributes are the winged cap and sandals, and the *caduceus,* or wand with two serpents twined about it. When the Romans came to Gaul, they found a powerful and widely-worshiped native divinity with some of the attributes familiar to them as Mercury's, but with others as well. Oversimplifying, they applied the name Mercury indifferently to the gods the Gauls distinguished as Teutates, "father of the tribe"; Esus, perhaps "master"; or Cernunnus, the god with stag's antlers.

The Romans would probably have identified as Mercury the little god in bronze plate, only sixteen-and-a-half inches high, found in 1845 at Bouray, and now in the St.-Germain-en-Laye museum (Fig. 6.3). His hair style is Roman, of the first Christian

6.3   St.-Germain-en-Laye, bronze god from Bouray

century. Everything else about the little god is Celtic: the torque, the strong chin, the low forehead, the eye inlaid in blue glass paste, the atrophied stag-legs, folded Buddha-fashion, such as we saw in the Roquepertuse statue (Fig. 1.13).

Quite another concept is to be seen in the reliefs labeled Esus and Tarvos Trigaranus, found in re-use under Nôtre-Dame-de-Paris, and now in the Cluny museum in Paris. Esus, represented as bearded, is chopping or trimming a tree with an ax (Fig. 6.4a). Tarvos Trigaranus is a splendid bull (Fig. 6.4b), with three cranes on his back; cranes were regarded, like Mercury, as guides to travelers. These reliefs were dedicated by the *nautae* of Paris in the reign of Tiberius (A.D. 14–37); the Romans had obviously as yet done nothing to stifle the artistic expression of Gallic concepts of their gods.

Still another concept of Esus is the so-called Mercury of Lezoux now at St.-Germain-en-Laye (Fig. 6.5). Though he wears the winged cap of the Roman Mercury, in every other respect he is the antithesis of that rather foppish youth. In the first place he is not a youth, but a solid, bearded, bourgeois Gaul in late middle age, wearing a hooded Gallic cloak, and carrying in his right hand a well-filled money bag, symbolizing the god's function as protector of trade. At his feet are a cock and a goat, both attributes of the Gallic Mercury. But an inscription names him Esus. Experts date him in the first Christian century.

Our next Mercury comes from a sixty-nine-piece silver treasure, dedicated to Mercury, found in 1830 at Berthouville, and now in the Cabinet des Médailles of the Bibliothèque Nationale in Paris. It is a silver-gilt cup (Fig. 6.6), probably Greek work of the first or second Christian centuries. It portrays the god in a rustic sanctuary, with a complete collection of attributes: caduceus, tortoise, purse, cock, and goat. An inscription records its dedication by a lady with a Graeco-Roman name: Julia Sibylla. The treasure was found in the ruins of a sanctuary. The owner of the land on which the sanctuary stood did his best to demolish

6.4a   Paris, altar, Esus face

what was left of the shrine, in the hope of finding more treasure,
but it was still possible for later excavators to make out the plan.
In its first phase, the temple stood in the northwest corner of a

TARVOS TRIGARANVS

6.4b   Paris altar, Tarvos Trigaranus

large court. It was destroyed in the invasions of A.D. 276 which caused the treasure to be hidden. In the second phase, Mercury's temple was rebuilt, and a second temple was added, dedicated

6.5   St.-Germain-en-Laye, Mercury of Lezoux

probably to his mother Maia, who had already been represented
in the treasure by cups, busts, and inscriptions.

Somehow related to the Roman Mercury was the stag-horned

6.6   Berthouville treasure, Mercury at shrine

Cernunnus, splendidly rendered on a funeral relief in Reims; the
photograph (Fig. 6.7) is of a cast in St.-Germain-en-Laye. The
bearded god sits cross-legged, in the Buddha pose, his antlers
spreading wide above his head. He wears the Gallic torque, and
a bracelet on his upper right arm. Cradled in his left arm is a
large bag, from which he is dispensing round objects—fodder or
money—to a diminutive bull and stag at his feet. The bag is an
attribute of the Gallic Mercury, but a Graeco-Roman Mercury
stands at Cernunnus' left, and an Apollo with a lyre at his right.
By the latter part of the second Christian century, when this relief was carved, the Gallic and Roman versions of the same divin-

6.7   Reims, Cernunnus (cast)

ity could stand side by side. The mouse or rat in the pediment is
a Gallic underworld symbol, which is how we know that this was
a funerary monument.

The Gauls liked to build their sanctuaries to their Mercury on
hilltops or peaks. Three may be mentioned by way of illustration.
The earliest and most famous, that of Mercury Dumias, was at
the top of the Puy-de-Dôme, in the department of the same name,
4,872 feet above sea level, from which on a clear day one can

see Mont Blanc. It was reached by a road with daring hairpin turns, which the Romans built, but the sanctuary, like the hilltop oppidum of Mt. Beuvray, must have been in use from pre-Roman times. On the very summit, amid the ruins of the chapel of St. Barnabé, is a platform on which a famous colossal statue of Mercury was built in Nero's reign. The sculptor was a Greek named Zenodotus, who had also fashioned a colossus of Nero in Rome. The Mercury was ten years in the making, and cost the equivalent of $2,000,000. Thirty meters below the peak, to the south, at the top of a series of terraces, was the temple, excavated between 1872 and 1878, when an observatory was being built on the summit. On the terrace just below the temple, facing south, five semicircular exedras were built, with seats where pilgrims might rest and admire the view. The temple was massively built of enormous blocks of local stone, set without mortar, and held together with clamps. The roof was of lead. The excavators reported finding revetments in over fifty different kinds of marble, as many as on the Palatine Hill in Rome. The aim of all this grandeur was no doubt to console the Arverni for the prestige they had lost when their leader Vercingetorix was defeated. Among the miscellaneous finds was a large number of goat horns, the goat being, as we saw, associated with Mercury. In Christian times the goat was associated with the devil, and in the Middle Ages witches were supposed to travel by broom to the Puy-de-Dôme on St. John's Eve to celebrate a Black Mass. The chapel of St. Barnabé was built as a Christian counterblast to His Satanic Majesty.

A second peak-sanctuary of Mercury existed from pre-Roman times at Donon, 2,418 feet above sea-level. Here over thirty *stelae* with dedications to Mercury were found. There were three temples on the summit, one of them, from the second Christian century, roofed with stone slabs instead of tiles. Just before World War II a column was erected nearby bearing a reconstruction, from fragments found on the site, of a Jupiter-giant group like the one here illustrated (Fig. 6.8) from the museum of Épinal. In

6.8   Épinal, Jupiter and giant

these groups, peculiar to the Rhineland, Jupiter as a horseman rides down a giant symbolizing barbarism, or the forces of the underworld. Some scholars see in the giant a Gallic Mercury conceived as a sinister god of the realms below. Near the Donon temples there is also a well-like cavity that has been taken as the tomb of a hero worshiped here along with Mercury. In front of the stone-roofed temple a relief of a god who is not Mercury was found in 1936. It illustrates the complexity of trying to relate Gallic concepts of gods to the Roman: this god wears a lion skin like Hercules, but instead of a club he carries an ax, like Esus; he wears a sword, like Mars, and his right hand rests on the horns of a stag, which reminds us of Cernunnus. Perhaps he personifies the Vosges Mountains, in which the Donon sanctuary stands.

The third and southernmost peak-sanctuary stands at 3,280 feet (1,000 meters) above sea-level at Châtelard-de-Lardiers, near Banon, thirty miles east of Carpentras, and on the road to Vaison. The summit is surrounded by a double wall enclosing twenty acres; on a terrace between the walls was the sanctuary, within a precinct measuring 115 by 65 feet. Inside the precinct wall was found an enormous deposit of 15,000 gold, silver, and bronze rings, placed there as votive offerings. There were also 50,000 tiny lamps, which would not burn for longer than an hour; they were lit by ancient worshipers as modern ones light a candle before the altar of their patron saint, who, at Le Châtelard, may well have been Mercury, patron of travelers. Since no coins were found later than the Antonines (Faustina the Younger, wife of Marcus Aurelius; she died about A.D. 175), we must suppose that after that date the god proved powerless to protect travelers against brigands.

After Mercury, Caesar names Apollo. Two of Apollo's great shrines in Gaul were at Sanxay and Grand. Sanxay, in its attractive and solitary riverside setting of plowland, meadow, and copse, is the most complete and original Gallic sanctuary yet excavated. The air photograph, in which north is to the right (Fig. 6.9) shows, for example, a temple of unique plan, oriented to the points of the compass, in the middle of a 208 by 190-foot portico on the topmost of three terraces leading up from the Vonne River. The center of its plan was a circular domed cella just under 30 feet in

6.9   Sanxay, air view

diameter, from which four wings project precisely north, south, east, and west. A further projection to the east marks a monumental approach. On the east side, holes made by stone-robbers indicate the emplacement of sixty-six columns, Composite or Corinthian, Hadrianic in date (A.D. 117–138); but finds of Gallic coins suggest that the sanctuary was in use, in a less ornate phase, before the Roman conquest. The air photograph also indicates the buttresses which supported the terrace on the side where the ground slopes toward the river. A fragmentary inscription in large letters has been restored to suggest that the sanctuary was dedi-

cated to Apollo, but bronze statuettes of Mercury and of Attis—
the consort of the Asiatic Mother-Goddess Cybele—were also
found, as well as a small Venus in terracotta. A vaulted tunnel
with room for a man to walk comfortably upright, leading from
the edge of the cella to the southeast corner of the portico, has
been interpreted as a device whereby concealed priests might work
from underground an ostensible oracle of Apollo.

The sanctuary was a place of pilgrimage, and the long parallel
lines on the air photograph, south and southeast of the temple
portico, indicate the site of inns for pilgrims.

The grassy space between the temple precinct and the baths
(covered with a modern roof) further east is the area of the middle
terrace. It contained porticoes on the south and east where pilgrims
might sleep while awaiting miraculous cures from the god, for
Apollo could heal as well as prophesy. In the middle of this terrace
excavators found a *tholos,* or round building, twenty-four feet in
diameter, the roof supported by fourteen columns. Such tholoi
were commonly erected in antiquity over the tomb of a hero—a
mortal, perhaps a chief, worshiped as superhuman after his death.

Baths occupied the buttressed terrace nearest the river. The
excavators distinguished three phases. The earliest, Hadrianic, is
the furthest east, closest to the river. It contained a pool with three
apses for tubs; behind these was a circular hot plunge, the *calidar-
ium,* an octagonal tepid bath, the *tepidarium,* and a square cold
pool, the *frigidarium.* Four small chambers north of these, two of
them heated, may have been dressing-rooms. West of this installation, in a second phase, a whole new set of baths was built; perhaps, in this period, one set was reserved for men, the other for
women. Still further west, in the third phase, another pool and the
exercise ground were added. From the northeast corner of the
baths a vaulted corridor led to a building with nineteen cubicles,
perhaps a house of prostitution. Local legend hints that the corridor, when found in the nineteenth century, was adorned with in-
decent frescoes, piously destroyed by the excavator, a priest.

Across the Vonne, south of the baths, the air photograph clearly shows a theater-amphitheater built into the side of the valley, with the masonry substructure for the lower seats. The building is 295 feet wide, the completely round arena 123 feet; the stage building (rectangle on the right) is unusually small—only 13 by 30 feet. The structure will have been used for religious pageants, and perhaps also for assemblies of the local tribe, the Pictones. A Roman road leads up to it from the northeast; it has been calculated that there was parking space near it for up to 2,000 wagons.

Grand, the other Apollo sanctuary to be discussed, is nowadays a little village of 600 souls, perched 1,312 feet up on a bare plateau in the Vosges mountains, a dozen miles southwest of Domrémy, the birthplace of Joan of Arc. In antiquity it was an important center on the frontier between the provinces of Gaul and Belgium, with what was described in the fourth century of our era as the most beautiful temple in the world; it also has the largest figured mosaic in Europe. (The title of largest geometric mosaic [2000 m²] is claimed for one in Constanta, Romania, the ancient Tomis.) Its rampart encloses an area of 3,280 by 1,148 feet.

The "most beautiful" temple lies within the rampart, under the village, but recent digging for a water main has unearthed its precinct wall, as well as a charming head of a baby, identified as the Severan prince Geta, who grew up to be assassinated, in A.D. 212, by his brother, the Emperor Caracalla. Caracalla came to Grand to take the cure, the function of the sanctuary having been as much medical as religious; it may be to him that the monumental aspect of the town is due. That the sanctuary was Apollo's is confirmed by a dedication to the god, found in 1935, in which the dedicator states that he performs this pious act "instructed by a dream": this suggests that Grand was a place of "incubation," like Sanxay, where sleeping patients were visited by the god in nocturnal visions. Apollo was worshiped here under the cult title of Grannus, from which the modern town takes its name.

Adjoining the temple is the basilica (120 by 72 feet) with its huge mosaic, over 45 feet square. The central panel represents a shepherd with his crook, conversing with another person, perhaps in a scene from comedy. The corners bear representations of animals: a dog, a leopard, a panther, and a boar; the rest is geometric, with a shield pattern in the apse, which adds 28 by 18 feet to the dimensions. The walls were revetted with white and polychrome marble. The roof was of oak and pine planking: their charred remains, from a fourth-century destruction, were found on the mosaic floor. The main north-south street, running parallel to the basilica, and the paving of what was probably the Forum, were discovered in 1962.

Just south of the rampart wall was an amphitheater, or rather a demi-amphitheater, one half having probably been occupied by stage buildings. Its 450-foot axis makes it longer than those of either Arles or Nîmes, and underlines the importance of the sanctuary as a place of pilgrimage in antiquity. Here in A.D. 309 the future Emperor Constantine saw a portent of victory and longevity: laurel crowns and crosses (XXX) in the sky, promising a thirty-year reign. This anticipated his vision, three years later, at the Mulvian Bridge near Rome, of the cross and crown—the *labarum*—which accompanied a heavenly voice crying *In hoc signo vinces* ("In this sign thou shalt conquer").

In Caesar's list of important Gallic divinities Mars comes next. I cite four sanctuaries which have demonstrable connections with Mars. The earliest (on the evidence of Gallic coins) is at Allonnes, near Le Mans, where the famous twenty-four-hour auto race is held annually in June. Here, a fragment of a circular monument, 30 feet in diameter, rises near the center of a perfectly oriented galleried precinct, about 330 feet square. Périgueux and Sanxay are other examples of round temples in square precincts. The round monument is known locally as the Fairies' Tower: according to legend a blue-eyed, raven-haired Roman empress called

Bella, who died of snake-bite, appears here at night diaphanously clad. No Mars cult here; but in 1959 two altars were found near the tower which were dedicated to Mars with the cult-title Mullo, possibly a derivation from the Celtic word for heap. Caesar states that the Gauls heap up high piles of the spoils of successful battles, as a trophy offered to Mars: footings in front of the temple may mark the spot where such trophies were heaped. An inscription by a Roman centurion adds to the martial tone, and a Corinthian capital of a size appropriate to a 23-foot column shows how massive the sanctuary buildings were. More puzzling is a column-drum bearing a relief of a wingless Cupid (?) flogging a naked man with his hands tied behind his back, for flogging normally goes with fertility cults, not with Mars. The sculptured head of a sick old woman, with sunken eyes, lined face, and tortured mouth, suggests that pilgrims came here to be cured of disease. Coins of Claudius, dated A.D. 51–54, and of Nerva, from A.D. 96–98, found sealed under a third-century floor, show that the sanctuary was in operation in the first Christian century; the latest coins, of Constantius II (351-361) show when it succumbed to barbarian invasion or Christian wrath. With the temple fell also the baths and the theater, amenities which we saw also at Sanxay.

The second in date of our four Mars sanctuaries is in Brittany, at Haut-Bécherel-en-Corseul; the name incorporates that of the Coriosolites, one of the tribes which resisted Caesar in 56 B.C. The spot is marked on Roman maps as Fanum Martis, "Shrine of Mars"; the identification is confirmed by a crude scrawl, mentioning a *simulacrum* or statuette of Mars, on a tile published in 1956. The tile was found in the portico of an oriented precinct like those at Sanxay and Allonnes, with a polygonal tower centered at the back of the west side. The coins range in date from Augustus to Constantine.

Our last two Mars sanctuaries are of roughly the same date, about the middle of the second Christian century. One is at Moulin-du-Fâ, two and a half miles northeast of Royan, a most at-

tractive watering-place at the mouth of the Gironde. The abandoned windmill from which the place takes its name is built in the
middle of the massive podium, 16 feet above the present ground
level, of a circular temple 118 feet in diameter. An inscription
found nearby, the only one found on the site, bears a dedication
to Mars. At the entrance, near a flight of stairs on the east, there is
a stone basin in which pilgrims washed their feet before entering
the temple, barefooted. The cella was paved and revetted with
polychrome marble, surrounded by a marble colonnade, and embellished with statues, of which four rectangular bases remain. Four
wells, perhaps of unexplained ritual significance, and of uncertain
date, pierce the cella floor. What is worth noting here is the elegance of Roman architecture and décor of the best period, applied
to a sanctuary of Gallic plan and Gallic religious significance.

Our fourth Mars sanctuary is at Villards-d'Héria, 2,644 feet up,
in an Alpine landscape of pines and bare rock, nowadays much
frequented for winter sports. The sanctuary falls into two sections, a kilometer apart. One overlooks the Lac d'Antre, at the
spot where a subterranean river gushes out of the ground to fall
into the lake below. An inscription guarantees the association with
Mars. There are several buildings in a walled precinct. The blocks
of the temple, laid without mortar and secured with clamps, were
found built into an adjoining farmhouse. There are in fact two
temples, as well as a building rich with red and green porphyry
and Egyptian granite, and possibly a theater. Among the finds
are fragments of a bronze religious calendar, very like the one
found at nearby Coligny; they record the festivals of the second
fortnight of the fifth Gallic month, called Ogron-, and corresponding to our November.

The other half of the sanctuary is built on arches over the
Héria brook, a kilometer to the west. It was dedicated to Mars'
consort Bellona, by an Aeduan who was priest at the sanctuary of
the Three Gauls at Lyon. Nearby were baths, with bricks bearing
stamps of the mid-second century of our era, and possibly an am-

phitheater. Behind the Roman Mars lurks the god of the Sequani, Segomo. Here this powerful tribe worshiped, under a borrowed name, their everyday god, on whom they had come to feel they could depend.

Jupiter, the supreme god of the Romans, ranks only fourth in Caesar's list of Gallic gods, and indeed Jupiter's sanctuaries in Gaul, apart from the official Roman *Capitolia* in the large towns, are not numerous. One, somewhat unusual, stands apart from any large settlement, at Vernègues, near Salon in Provence (a town notorious as the birthplace of the sixteenth-century astrologer Nostradamus), in a ghost-village destroyed by an earthquake in 1909 and never rebuilt. The central temple, perfectly Roman in style, a little smaller than the Maison Carrée in Nimes but of about the same date, stands at the top of a monumental flight of twenty steps in a semicircular precinct 213 feet in diameter. A dedication to Jupiter Tonans ("the Thunderer") guarantees the ascription. The west wall (Fig. 6.10) is intact, with a Corinthian pilaster and one Corinthian column 23 feet tall. To the right of the temple traces of another one have been found; in the interests of the symmetry to which the Romans were addicted, there should have been a third on the other side; the set would have been dedicated to the Capitoline triad, Jupiter, his consort Juno, and his daughter Minerva. Sets of three temples of this kind are rare, but examples are known in Sbeïtla (Roman Sufetula) in Tunisia, and in Bolonia (Roman Baelo) in southern Spain. The remarkable thing about the Vernègues temple is how little Gallic it is; Camille Jullian has well described it as "a provincial espisode of Hellenistic art."

Last on Caesar's list comes the smith-god Vulcan. A Vulcan sanctuary has been identified at La Motte du Ciar, just southwest of the cathedral city of Sens. The most noteworthy thing about it is the taste it evinces for the colossal. The precinct is a huge

6.10   Vernègues, temple of Jupiter

twenty-five-acre rectangle, oriented north and south, with a vast
apse in the middle of its long west side. The rectangle measures
1300 by 650 feet; the Place de la Concorde in Paris covers only
two-thirds the area. The apse, 725 feet wide and 558 feet deep,
would comfortably contain Sens cathedral, one of the longest of
Gothic buildings; the Gallo-Roman apse covers twenty times the
area of Nôtre-Dame-de-Paris. Centered in the apse were found
the footings of a semicircular building of 248 by 213 feet, with
rectangular annexes on each side, and weepholes in the floor to
allow the concrete to "breathe." It may represent the foundations
of a tower, as at Sanxay and Périgueux; if so, the tower was the
victim of medieval stone-robbing.

The toe from a colossal bronze statue, in the Sens museum, is
of a size to match the hugeness of the sanctuary: it measures

seven inches, which means the statue it came from was thirty-three feet tall. A huge inscription, forty feet long, also in the Sens museum, was found in re-use in the south front of the late city wall, the side facing toward the sanctuary. It is of exactly the size to fit over the sanctuary's main (east) entrance. It is a dedi-cation, to Vulcan among others, by a rich and distinguished citizen of Sens (Roman Agedincum)—he boasts that he has been *flamen* (sacrificer-priest) of Augustus, and has held all the municipal of-fices. Because of the dedication to Vulcan, it has been conjectured that he was a prosperous proprietor of a metalworks, as rich as C. Julius Rufus, who paid for the Lyon amphitheater and the Saintes arch. A coin of Domitian found in the floor of the build-ing in the apse gives the earliest possible date (A.D. 81–96) for the sanctuary, but the taste for the colossal is more characteristic of the second century, Hadrianic or later.

One of the most striking aspects of Gallic religion was the im-portance attached to healing springs. We have already seen how the water god Nemausus gave Nimes its name. Another important water sanctuary, dated by a coin hoard (Augustus-Domitian) in the first Christian century, was at Fontaines-Salées, by St.-Père-sous-Vézelay. Tourists visiting the great twelfth-century abbey should also visit the temple and baths on the plain to the south. The Roman ruins appear in old French epic poetry as a castle; in modern times the local priest became interested in them, and choirboys would whip off their surplices after mass and go to work with pick and shovel, to remove the earth with which the salt-springs area was covered in the fourteenth century, to prevent the peasants from evading the salt-tax. Remains in the area go back to prehistoric times: some of the fire-hollowed oak logs with which the wells were lined have a carbon-14 date of 2970 B.C. ± 200, the cremation necropolis is of 1000 B.C., and there are earthworks and a chariot-road dating from the fourth or third century B.C. The sanctuary proper consists of a large temple in its precinct, 165 feet wide, visible in the lower right corner of the air photograph, Fig. 6.11; there is an elaborate set of baths adjoining. In the temple storeroom a number of stone models was discovered representing the part of the body the patient wanted cured: a hand, a foot, a thigh, a penis. The finds from Fontaines-Salées are divided between the site-museum and the museum thirty miles to the north in Auxerre.

The baths went through four phases. To the earliest, from the first Christian century, belong the round room with the radiant-heating ducts and latrines in the adjoining quarter round, plus the square paved pool, all visible in the left center (north) of the air photograph. The second phase is probably Hadrianic. Hadrian decreed that men and women should bathe separately; hence a new round warm pool, designed to support a cupola, was added to the south. The rest of the complex belong to this phase. The long room in the east wing (near the center of the air photograph) may have been the dormitory where patients hoped to be visited by the heal-

6.11   Fontaines-Salées, air view

ing god in dreams. The smaller rooms in this wing had glazed picture-windows and frescoes; they may have been beauty parlors, since hairpins, palettes for mixing cosmetics, perfume-vases, handles of cosmetic-boxes, and little spoons for extracting wax from the ears were found there. South of the portico are the openings of the wood-lined therapeutic wells. This phase was destroyed in A.D. 186 by a marauding band of deserters under one Maternus. It was rebuilt, and this third phase lasted till the barbarian invasions of 276. The square orifices in the round precinct (air photograph, upper right quadrant) belong to the sanctuary's fourth and final phase, dated by coins as ranging from Constantius II (A.D. 324) to Arcadius (394–408). Fruit-pits and nuts represent all the poverty-stricken pilgrims could afford to offer.

A second important water sanctuary, at St.-Germain-Sources-Seine, was in use for over four centuries, from the reign of Claudius (A.D. 41–54) to that of Maximus (383–388). The actual source of the Seine is the property of the city of Paris, and was embellished—if that is the word—in 1867 with an artificial grotto and an equally artificial nymph, both now much delapidated. The sanctuary, about a mile north of the source, centers on a spring, a peristyle on a terrace, a pool, and a temple. Inscriptions show that the goddess Sequana was worshiped there, and that pilgrims slept in her precinct in hope of a cure. Faith was the moving force, since the water has no medicinal qualities. Dedications of parts of the body have long been known, and replicas of eyes, breasts, sexual organs, heads, hands, knees and feet found at this sanctuary are on display at the Dijon museum. There are also representations of cretins and lepers, of patients suffering from tumor and blindness, goiter, hernia, breast cancer, and arthritis, as well as reliefs or statues of pilgrims making offerings of purses of money, vases, goblets, hares, chickens, a bunch of grapes (this is the Burgundy wine-country), and a child offering a puppy. In 1933 a statuette of Sequana was found; she wears a crown and stands, with a gesture of welcome, in a boat whose figurehead is a swan with a fruit in its beak (Fig. 6.12). The most interesting find of all was made in the sanctuary pool in 1963: 190 representations in wood of parts of the body (Fig. 6.13), some highly anatomical and including, for instance, a thorax closed and an-

6.12   Dijon, Sequana, from St.-Germain-Sources-Seine

6.13   St.-Germain-Sources-Seine, wooden *ex-votos*
       as found

other open. It took excavators a difficult week to extract them from
the mud in which they were imbedded. A sherd of Claudius' reign,
stuck to one of them, provided a date in the mid-first century of
our era. Similar dedications, of the same period, were found in the
sanctuary of Montbouy, together with four vast hoards of coins,
totaling 9,351 pieces, buried during the troubles of the third and
fourth centuries. Another lot of wooden figures, of later date
(second and third centuries), comes from the sanctuary at
Essarois, also near the source of the Seine: it includes representations of pregnant women and swaddled babies. There is a cultural
continuity between offerings such as we have been discussing and
Christian shrines like Lourdes or Ste.-Anne-de-Beaupré.

Our final example of a water sanctuary is Chassenon, ancient
Cassinomagus ("Oakfield"), on the Roman road between Limoges and Saintes. Like other pilgrimage centers, it had its baths
and its theater-amphitheater, but more interesting are its temple
and an extensive series of underground settling basins. The temple,

twice the size of Sanxay, as big as the Tour de Vésone at Périgueux, is octagonal in plan, around a circular cella, with walls ten
feet thick to support a cupola. At the top of the monumental en-
trance-stair is a well, and centered just beyond are the footings of
an altar, found filled with horns of sacrificed animals, especially
the stag. The finds are divided between the small site-museum and
the museum of Rochechouart, four miles away. A wall with only
two narrow entrances, at the opening of the cella, blocks from
profane view the mysterious rites which went on within. Inside the
marble-paved and marble-revetted cella are the base for the cult
statue, another well (found empty), and a natural cleft in the rock,
which might have been used for the working of an oracle, as at
Delphi, or regarded as what the Romans called a *mundus,* a means
of communication between the world of the living and the underworld of the dead. The wells here are not confined to the temple:
the excavators report fifty more in the near environs, of which
thirty-one were examined, and found to contain Antonine coins
dated A.D. 138–192, animal bones, and vases, forty of them un-
broken: these, having been used once for sacrifice, were holy, and
not used again.

Some 200 yards east of the temple are the remarkable underground settling-basins, called locally the Caves de Longeas. They
underlie a 230 by 300-foot building, at least one of whose rooms
was hypocaust-heated; it stood in an enclosure measuring 720 by
1,120 feet, and may have contained facilities for ritual bathing.
Fig. 6.14a shows the aqueduct which served the complex;
Fig. 6.14b shows one of the twenty-seven vaulted settling-
basins. These were each over 21 feet high to the top of the
vault, and ranged in width from 6½ to 13 feet, in length from
22 to 54 feet. They were separated by walls averaging nine feet in
thickness, at the bottom of which are apertures averaging four feet
in height and five feet in width, cut on the diagonal to break the
flow of water and facilitate the deposit of silt and impurities.
The vaulted passages are arranged in blocks perpendicular to

6.14a   Chassenon, tunnel

6.14b   Chassenon, settling basin

each other, which could be closed off one at a time for repair and cleaning without cutting off the water supply altogether. The finds of coins show that the installation was in use from Claudius (A.D. 41–54) to Constantine (311–337). Here at Chassenon, where the full resources of Roman engineering skill were put at the disposal of a Gallic cult, we have a final impressive example of Roman official tolerance of native religion.

VII

Gallic Arts and Crafts

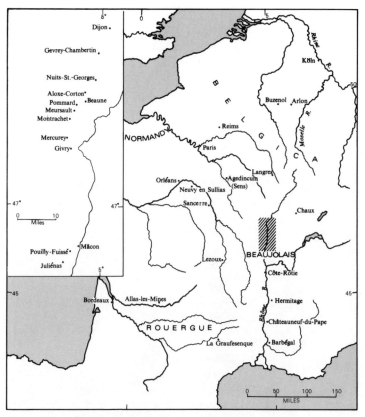

7.1   Map: findspots of reliefs, etc., illustrating arts
and crafts. (Inset: the Burgundy wine-country)

What archaeology has to tell us about Gallic arts and crafts would
be minimal were it not for Commandant Espérandieu's collection,
unique in the annals of science, of nearly 8,600 illustrations of
reliefs, statues, and busts illustrating private life in Roman Gaul,
published, with supplements, over a period of forty-eight years,
spanning two World Wars. The collection brings to life, largely
through grave-monuments, the work of artisans with an attitude
healthily different from that of the Roman establishment: pride
in manual labor.

When the inhabitants of Agedincum, nowadays Sens (see map,
Fig. 7.1) were threatened by barbarian invasion, probably in the
late third century of our era, they used whatever stones lay ready
to their hand, including sculptured grave-monuments, to build
an emergency wall. When this wall was dismantled, beginning in
1845, the stones became the nucleus of the local museum, which
thus contains the finest collection in France of illustrations of
artisans at work. One of these (Fig. 7.2) shows interior decorators

7.2   Sens, stuccoer at work, relief

producing the kind of craftsmanship in stucco and fresco which adorned rich town houses, and villas like Montmaurin. Two workmen are mounted on scaffolding supported by sawhorses. The one on the left holds a palette and brush, and is painting a wall; on one side of him is a bucket of brushes; on the other, a stool for reaching the top of the wall. To his right is a plasterer smoothing the wall with his trowel. At the foot of the scaffolding, to the right, a workman is mixing mortar. On a flight of stairs to the left an architect or overseer sits and consults plans. He is wearing the professional man's long gown; the other three are in workmen's short tunics.

Another stone from Sens is a draper's monument, in two scenes. The lower (Fig. 7.3a) represents a fuller at work. Formal Gallo-Roman dress required frequent washing and whitening, which was done by treading the clothes in vats filled with a mixture of water and urine. In our relief, the fuller is standing in his vat, working the impurities out of the cloth by jumping on it with his bare feet, giving himself purchase by supporting his arms on a pair of banisters fixed to the sides of the tub; behind him, a piece of cloth is thrown over a rod suspended by two rings from the ceiling. In the relief above (Fig. 7.3b), the draper, with a huge pair of shears, is cutting a length of cloth thrown over an easel-like arrangement whose transverse bar can be raised or lowered by adjusting pegs in the uprights.

A third monument portrays a smith, named Bellicus, the son of Bellator (Fig. 7.4). In his right hand he holds a hammer, in his left an iron bar resting on an anvil. Flanking him in low relief are two other tools of his trade, tongs to his left, a poker to his right. Since he is wearing only one shoe, the inference is that he was lame, as ancient smiths, beginning with their patron god, Vulcan, traditionally were. At his feet are two pets, a dog and a rabbit. His hair is close-cropped, save for one long lock; this hair style suggests that he was either a priest of Isis or a German: both affected this coiffure.

7.3a   Sens, fuller at work, relief

A grave relief from Reims (Fig. 7.5) shows a cobbler at work. He sits astride his bench, his last before him, his tools in a basket behind him, and in a rack within convenient reach on the wall.

7.3b   Sens, draper cutting cloth, relief

The Sens craftsmen were self-employed, on a small scale. The closest the Gauls came to large-scale enterprise was in the manufacture of pottery, chiefly at two centers, La Graufesenque and

7.4   Sens, smith, relief

Lezoux, which successively monopolized the market. Gallic pottery was an imitation of the molded, red-glazed ware called
Arretine, made at Arezzo in Italy, which derived its shapes and
motifs from more expensive silver.

The potter would line a stone mold with eight to ten millimeters
of clay, turn the mold on his wheel, attach a foot to his cup, and
then dip the pot by hand in a fine glaze containing ferrous oxide
and saltpeter, the clay kept in stable suspension by alkalizing
with sodium carbonate, such as can be obtained from wood ash.
The pot was then allowed to dry until leather-hard, after which
it was placed in the kiln and fired at a temperature of 1,050°
centigrade. The kiln was a two-storied affair. A wood fire

occupied the lower level; the upper had a perforated floor, the holes of which could be blocked with plugs to regulate the heat. Oxidation produced a fine sealing-wax-red glaze (Fig. 7.6); reduction produced black. In the oxidation process, the coals were raked out and the intense heat allowed to circulate in the vaulted

7.5   Reims, cobbler at work, relief

7.6   La Graufesenque: two bowls

upper chamber; in reduction, the fire was stoked with green wood, and the resulting smoke blackened the pots. The potters, proud of their work, signed their pots; 293 potters' stamps are known from La Graufesenque alone. The pots were distributed widely, even competing with Arretine ware in Italy. At Pompeii, destroyed by the eruption of Vesuvius in A.D. 79, the excavators found an unopened crate of ninety La Graufesenque pots.

Among the most interesting La Graufesenque discoveries was a series of potters' accounts scratched on sherds (Fig. 7.7). The accounts were kept in three columns: in the first, the potter's name, often Gallic; in the second, the pot type; in the third, the dimension and number of pots fired. A set of thirty-four accounts, all of the same date, but not all complete, published in 1923,

7.7   La Graufesenque: sherd with potter's accounts

added up to the amazing total of 868,000 pots; a single potter was responsible for as many as 150,000. About A.D. 85 the monopoly passed to Lezoux: a potter named Libertus, whose stamps are found in both places, emigrated with his trade secrets from La Graufesenque to Lezoux, which thereafter cornered the market.

Too few workshops have been excavated. One at Lezoux covered, with its drying area, 900 square meters. It had a tile floor, pits for storing the clay, and a small mill for grinding borax, one of the additives which imparted a fine gloss to the glaze. The excavator at Lezoux believed, as a result of experiments, that the pots were fired twice, once before glazing, once after. The kilns for the first firing were square or rectangular; for the second, round. Since kilns of the first type were four times as numerous as those of the second, he deduced that the second firing was a specialized business, involving jealously guarded trade secrets.

Closely related to the pottery industry was the art of glass blowing, for the glass workers borrowed their shapes—139 have been distinguished (Fig. 7.8)—from the potters. Molded glass had been known in the East since remote antiquity, but glass *blowing* was invented in Syria in the first century B.C., and Syrian experts soon immigrated to Rome's western provinces, setting up shop first in Provence, but soon establishing branches in the valleys of the Rhône, the Moselle, and the Rhine. The latter district, especially at Cologne* became a major center of the art. The best known French firm, that of Frontinus, had its headquarters in Normandy, and specialized in barrel-shaped bottles. By the third Christian century, glass blowers had learned to make glass colorless by adding manganese oxide, but they also made handsome colored glass, blue, green, purple, brown, yellow, and polychrome. Much plain Roman glass is more beautiful now than it was originally, because of the iridescence it acquires through being buried in the ground. By blowing the glass into wet wooden

*ROR, 207.

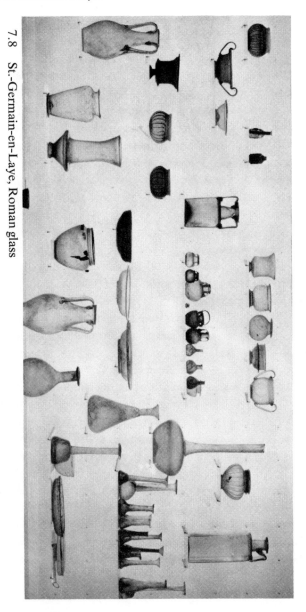

7.8 St.-Germain-en-Laye, Roman glass

molds the artisans produced prismatic shapes, square, hexagonal, ribbed, dimpled. Glass served a multitude of purposes. It held the ashes of the cremated dead. It supplied pitchers, carafes, mugs, goblets, drinking horns, funnels, footed drinking glasses, tumblers, nursing bottles, vials for perfume and bath oil, bowls, plates, flat-sided "pilgrim flasks" (the shape used nowadays for Franconian, Portuguese, and Chilean wine). Glass was molded into the shapes of fish, scallops, birds, a monkey playing a Pan-pipe, a bunch of grapes, a human head, a basket, a helmet, an hour glass. It was ornamented in *appliqué* with knobs, fish, charioteers, gladiators, serpentine patterns; it was paneled, cut undercut,* gilded, painted, inscribed.

The tradition of ancient glass blowing passed to Venice, and thrives now at Murano in the Venetian lagoon. Morin-Jean, the greatest French expert on Gallo-Roman glass, describes and illustrates (Fig. 7.9) the execution to his order, using the time-honored ancient methods, of a glass *kantharos*: a wine-cup with a deep bowl and a tall stem, two loop-shaped handles rising above the rim, attached to the rim and to the lower edge of the body. The final shape, which took thirty-five minutes to complete, appears at the lower right-hand corner of the drawing. The work-man picked up a mass of liquid glass on the end of his blowpipe (1), and hollowed it by blowing (2), then clipped it by turning it rapidly between pincers (3). An assistant then affixed an iron rod to the glass, opposite the blowpipe end, and detached the blowpipe (4). The glass bubble was then rotated, opened (5), and shaped (6, 7), the piece being frequently warmed at the kiln during the process. Next came the handles. With another iron rod, the assistant attached a blob of glass at the point where the upper end of the handle was to be attached (8). Then the blob was cut with scissors, thinned, curved with the pincers (9), and attached at the appropriate point at the bottom of the bowl (10).

*The famous *diatretae*: *Romans on the Rhine*, Fig. 7.20.

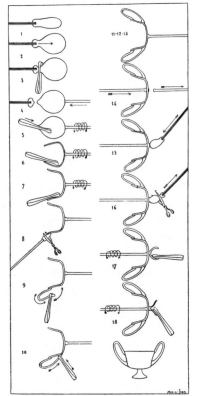

7.9   Steps in blowing a glass *cantharos*

The operation was repeated for the other handle (11-13). The
next step was to attach the foot. The workman affixed a new rod
to the interior of the vase (14), detaching the one he had used
during phases 4 to 13 of the operation. Meanwhile, another workman had attached another blob of blown glass to the base of the
bowl (15), and then cut off the blowpipe (16). The bowl was
then revolved, and the foot opened and enlarged to the desired
shape (17, 18).

Morin-Jean distinguished two periods of Roman glass in Gaul.

The first, Roman I, extended over the first two Christian centuries,
from Augustus to the Severan dynasty. In this period the natural
glass is blue-green, but comes also in strong colors. The shapes
were produced by blowing into molds of geometric shape. Squat
heavy flagons with angular handles are popular. The workshops
are concentrated in the Rhône valley. Roman II occupies the
period from 193 to 423, from the Severans to Honorius. Morin-
Jean subdivides it into two phases, the first running to about the
middle of the third century. This is the peak of the industry,
a Syrian specialty fostered by the Severans, who had Syrian
connections by marriage. The process of making colorless glass
with manganese oxide is invented; shapes are varied and elegant,
with delicate feet, long necks, and ornate handles. The plastic
shapes mentioned above (human and animal heads, bunches of
grapes, etc.) become popular, and spun glass is applied to the sur-
face in knobs, spirals, rolls, and leaves. Glass is cut, painted, and
gilded. The production centers are in the province of Belgica and
along the Rhine. The second phase of Roman II is decadent: the
glass is impure, cloudy, greenish or yellowish, showing bubbles
and streaks. Shapes are less sure, virtuosity exaggerated, decoration slovenly. Serpentine decoration in spun glass abounds; enamel
begins to be found. At the end of the period appear Christian
motifs, drawn from the Old and New Testament.

The technique of mosaic-making is related to workmanship in
glass: some mosaic tesserae *are* glass.* By 1913, 1,600 mosaics
were known in Roman Gaul, and Frenchmen working in Algiers
have added considerably to our knowledge of the mosaic-making
process. For example, they have noticed the use of color—as
many as thirty different shades—to give the effect of depth and
perspective. The mosaicist set no great store by realism in the
use of color: he had no hesitation in using red tesserae for leaves

---

*The process was described in *Romans on the Rhine* (210) and need not be
repeated *in extenso* here.

if green were unavailable. Color differentiated the sexes: men tanned, women pale.

Careful attention has been paid to the size of the tesserae used: larger ones (47 to 90 tesserae per 10 cm²) for geometric patterns, smaller ones for figures. For backgrounds, 63 to 163 tesserae per 10 cm², for figures, 66 to 288. The mosaicist arranged his pattern of tesserae in a box with a sliding top and bottom; when he slid out the bottom, the tesserae fell into the soft cement and were pressed in by an ironing process, with a kind of trowel called a "float," still used by plasterers and masons. Experiment showed that 40 cm² of tesserae could be laid at a time in this way; this, accordingly, was the optimum size of the box. An alternative method used a reverse pattern on cloth, with the size, number, and color of the tesserae indicated. Or the tesserae could be unrolled on fresh cement, and hammered in.

The French in Algiers also perfected a technique for taking up and preserving ancient mosaic pavements. They covered the tesserae with a cloth spread with glue, and placed a board above. They then undermined the cement in which the tesserae were fixed, slid a board below, tied the top and bottom boards together, and flipped them over. The mosaic was then made ready for display on the floor or wall of a museum. They note the importance of a mosaic as an archaeological seal: the mosaic is always later than the latest object found under it: it is therefore obviously important to note the date of coins and sherds so found. The technique of mosaic making is an obdurate one, a challenge, met proudly by the ancient masters, and recognized as different from the technique of painting. That the skill was mastered is proved by the mosaics of Ravenna, which come very late in antiquity, and are far from decadent.

Agriculture ranked with pottery-making as a major occupation of Roman Gaul. In a slave-based economy, there is little incentive to invent labor-saving devices; therefore two Gallo-Roman

mechanical contrivances are particularly worthy of notice. The
first is a mechanical reaper, portrayed (Fig. 7.10) on a grave
relief of A.D. 165-190, found in 1948 at Buzenol in Belgian
Luxembourg. What the relief shows is a box on wheels, with teeth
fixed in front which engage the grain ears, cut them off, and throw
them into the box. The device was about five feet wide, to fit the
country lanes. The motive power is a mule who pushes from
behind. Another relief (see sketch, Fig. 7.10), found in nearby
Arlon, completes the picture. It shows a man in the shafts behind
the mule; his function is to raise or lower the shafts in order to
regulate the height of the teeth to match the height of the standing grain. The function of the man in front is to free the teeth of

7.10   Buzenol, mechanical reaper, relief

grain. Obviously the device tended to jam, to waste grain, and to spoil the chaff, but it was practical on large estates in flat country. It is illustrated again in the seasons-reliefs in the arch of the Porte de Mars in Reims, and another example was reported from Trier in 1964. But it fell out of use in late antiquity, and was not re-invented until the nineteenth century. The Buzenol relief attracted wide attention, even being reproduced in *Life* in 1958. It is an example of Gallic ingenuity in the invention of wheeled vehicles: most of the names the Romans used for carts and wagons were Gallic. The English translations of the Gallic terms evoke a vanished age of horse-drawn transport: *benna,* trap (with wickerwork body); *carpentum,* buggy; *carruca,* coach; *cisium,* cabriolet; *petorritum,* four-wheeler; *pilentum,* surrey; *sarracum,* dray. The Gauls also invented the wheeled plow, and showed their ingenuity in agricultural matters by their use of organic fertilizers and their probable invention of the scythe. On the artistic side, the various reliefs portraying the reaper are of interest as proving the existence of traveling sculptors who included local motifs in their pattern-books.

The other interesting Gallo-Roman mechanical contrivance is the aqueduct-fed water mill, of the third Christian century, at Barbegal, which dominates the solitude of the *maquis* near Arles (Fig. 7.11). The total rise is sixty-nine feet above the marsh; the 30° grade gave the architect a two-hundred foot slope to work with. To take full advantage of his space, he designed parallel rows of roofed mills, two sets of eight races each, sixty-five feet wide overall, with a service tunnel between. The mill wheels were over seven feet in diameter, and of the bucket or overshot type, waterproofed with linseed oil and manganese dioxide. Their axle engaged a toothed vertical wheel which in turn engaged a horizontal toothed drum which turned the grinding wheel. The excavator calculated that the mill would produce from 500 to 700 pounds of grain an hour, or, in a ten-hour day, a minimum of two and a half tons, which would feed 80,000 people. We

7.11   Barbegal, water-mill

know the name of the architect: his sarcophagus lies in the ancient cemetery of the Alyscamps in Arles. He was Q. Candidius
Benignus, modest, kindly, called "master" by master craftsmen,
"for none surpassed him in the art of constructing machines and
watercourses."

The growing of grapes, especially in France, is an important
subdivision of agriculture, and no book on Roman France would
be complete without some discussion of the Gallo-Roman origins

of the great bottlings of our time. They certainly go back to the first century of our era, for the Emperor Domitian, after a year of poor grain harvest and good vintage (perhaps A.D. 93), decreed the uprooting of half the vines in the province. However, he did not enforce the edict, and the canny Gauls no doubt continued to grow grapes, concealing the prosperity of their vineyards as far as possible from the cupidity of the imperial tax collectors. The hero of French winegrowers should be the Emperor Probus (A.D. 276-282), who permitted *all* Gauls to cultivate the vine, which implies that before his reign *some* could. The modern French wines with the oldest ancestry appear to be those of the Côtes du Rhône: Côte Rotie, Hermitage, and Châteauneuf-du-Pape. Burgundies are mentioned as early as A.D. 312. There were Gallo-Roman vineyards along the north-south line which makes the journey from Dijon to Mâcon a pilgrimage for wine lovers—at Gevrey-Chambertin, Vougeot, Vosne-Romanée, Nuits-St.-Georges, Aloxe-Corton, Beaune, Pommard, Meursault, Montrachet, Mercurey, and Givry. Beaujolais goes back to the same period at Pouilly-Fuissé and Juliénas, and we are told that Roman soldiers did the planting at Loire vineyards like Sancerre. The professor-poet Ausonius, about A.D. 371, praised the wines both of the Moselle and of his native Bordeaux. Areas not now particularly famous for viticulture flourished in Roman France. For example, in 1964 were published the results of excavating a winery at Allas-les-Mines. It had eleven rooms, including one for treading grapes, and one with a wine press. It flourished from Flavian times (A.D. 69-96) to Tetricus, who ruled in Aquitania from A.D. 270 to 274. The vine was cultivated commercially in the latitude of Paris from the reign of Julian (A.D. 361-363) to the 1914 war. The great chestnut forests like Fontainebleau were originally planted to protect the vines. Reliefs and sarcophagi show details of the vintage: men on ladders pruning and gathering grapes, putting them in baskets and treading and pressing them. A relief in Langres (Fig. 7.12) shows an enormous wine

7.12   Langres, wine-wagon, relief

barrel on a four-wheeled wagon drawn by two mules, head down. struggling hard under the heavy load. A relief in Dijon (Fig. 7.13) shows a wineshop. The bar is very high, taller than a man, to keep customers from helping themselves. The boy tending bar holds a wine measure in each hand; others, in graduated sizes, hang on hooks behind him. He is pouring the wine, through a funnel set in the bar, into a jug which a customer is holding up. The bar is equipped with three such spigots, each with a basin below to catch the drip. Next door is a delicatessen or butcher shop, with a curly-headed child in charge. Sausages hang in clusters over his head. Beside the counter is a chopping block and cleaver; in front of it, a tub of lard.

Gallo-Romans anticipated the modern French taste for apéritifs in their fondness for blending wine with such substances as absinthe, myrtle, rose water, oil of cedar, cinnamon, and even sea water. They were particularly fond of resinated wine, which is still a Greek taste. The extraction of resin was a minor industry, which flourished particularly in the pine forests of the Rouergue, in the department of Aveyron, not far north of La Graufesenque. The collecting of resin was incidental to cutting wood for the pottery kilns: the resin was obtained not by tapping, but by distillation from pinewood. The workmen buried a large jar,

7.13   Dijon, wine shop, relief

sometimes as much as a meter high, in the earth, put a wooden grill over it, and covered it with another, filled with pine boughs and turned upside down. The gap between the jars was sealed with clay, and a fire lit round the upper jar. The combustion gases escaped through a hole in the bottom of the upper jar, the distilled resin collected in the lower. Besides its use for flavoring wine, the resin served for caulking ships and making torches.

Of Gallo-Roman professions for which there is archaeological evidence, perhaps the most interesting is that of the ophthalmologist. The evidence consists of mortars for the preparation of eye salve, and numerous stamps used to impress on blocks of salve the formula of the prescription and the name of the doctor prescribing it. The Gauls and Germans appear to have been particularly subject to diseases of the eye: ten times as many of these stamps are known from Gaul and Germany as from Britain. The salve was put up in two-inch sticks. The kit of an ophthalmologist named C. Firmius Severus, dated by coins to the Antonine period (A.D. 138-180), found in Reims in 1854 and now in the St.-Germain-en-Laye museum, held forty grains of salve containing myrrh and beeswax, used for conjunctivitis. There was also an apothecary's scale, and nineteen tools of the trade, including four wooden bowls, a mortar, a cauterizer, a spatula with an olive-shaped end, tenterhooks, tweezers, scalpels with damascened handles, and an instrument for removing cataracts. The salves—and the doctors as well—usually bear Greek names. The ingredients include horn, ivy, balsam, copper, rose water, amber, saffron, vervain; oxides, peroxides, or carbonates of lead, iron, calcium, silica, and copper; opium, and white pepper! One stamp is four-sided, for four different prescriptions. The stamps sometimes include directions for mixing the salve, with egg white, water, sweet wine, or mother's milk; for the means of application, a sponge or brush; and the disease for which the salve is specific, trachoma, scarred cornea, pinkeye, rheumy secretions, burns, or cataract.

Finally, a word about the practice of the plastic arts, and particularly of sculpture in bronze. An especially fine set of bronzes was found by workmen in 1861 in a sandpit at Neuvy-en-Sullias just south of the Loire fifteen miles upstream from Orléans; they are now in the Orléans museum. They formed part of a temple treasure, hidden in a hastily constructed room in a time of invasion. The most impressive find is a spirited bronze horse (Fig. 7.14), with detachable mane and bridle; the base is equipped with

7.14 Neuvy-en-Sullias, bronze horse

four bronze rings through which poles could be slipped for carrying the animal in procession; he weighs just under 120 pounds. The base also bears an inscription, to a hitherto un-

known deity, Rudiobus, who may be a horse god, or a cult title
for Mars or Apollo. Other animal statues include some splendid
boars (Fig. 7.15), a short-legged stag with detachable horns,
and a bull, who has unfortunately lost his head. But the pieces
which speak most directly to modern taste are human: a running
man, a tightrope-walker, a dancer, and particularly a *danseuse*
(Fig. 7.16), less than four inches high, but full of verve and taut
vitality. One can easily understand why these masterpieces, with

7.15   Neuvy-en-Sullia, bronze boar

their virtuosity, competence, ease, and elegance, caused a sensation when they were exhibited in Paris in 1955. They are native
Gallic work, and they are dated in the first Christian century. The
temple treasure included sacrificial bowls, and a bronze trumpet
nearly five feet long. It is tempting to connect all this with the
central sanctuary of the Druids, which is known to have been
somewhere near Orléans.

7.16 Neuvy-en-Sullias, bronze statuette of *danseuse*

VIII

Roman-Inspired Architecture
in Modern France

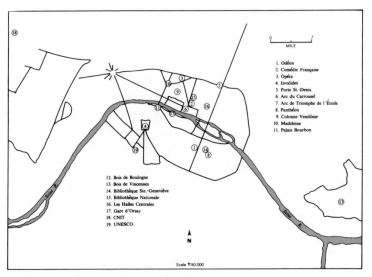

1. Odéon
2. Comédie Française
3. Opéra
4. Invalides
5. Porte St.-Denis
6. Arc du Carrousel
7. Arc de Triomphe de l'Étoile
8. Panthéon
9. Colonne Vendôme
10. Madeleine
11. Palais Bourbon

12. Bois de Boulogne
13. Bois de Vincennes
14. Bibliothèque Ste.-Geneviève
15. Bibliothèque Nationale
16. Les Halles Centrales
17. Gare d'Orsay
18. CNIT
19. UNESCO

8.1   Paris, plan, with location of Roman-inspired
        monuments

211

The latest Roman-inspired building thus far described is Sidonius Apollinaris' villa on Lac Aydat, of A.D. 460-65. Sidonius was a Christian bishop, and it is ironically significant that it was the Christianity which the Roman emperors had once persecuted that kept Roman literary and architectural traditions alive through the Dark Ages and beyond.

Sidonius died in about 479. Only seventeen years later, Clovis, the Frankish tribal chief who founded the French Merovingian dynasty, was baptized at Reims, and adjured, "Worship what you have burned, and burn what you have worshiped." He did: he founded the abbey of Ste.-Geneviève just north of what had been the Forum of Roman Paris.*

Charlemagne (768-814) was Roman emperor as well as Frankish king; his chapel at Aachen derives from the Graeco-Roman (Byzantine) architecture in Ravenna. He revived Latin learning: his courtiers called each other by Latin nicknames, and Latin was the language of his court. Shortly after Charlemagne's time, French feudal manors began to rise on the sites of Roman villas.

"Romanesque" architecture, which flourished *ca.* 1050-1150, is well named: its basilica-plans, round and superimposed arches, barrel vaults, geometrical forms and volumes, and Corinthian capitals speak a Roman architectural language. The cathedral of Angoulême, dating from 1105, for instance, has its nave roofed with domes like the Pantheon in Rome. We shall see the same technique used again in the nineteenth century for the Madeleine in Paris.

It would be idle to pretend that Gothic architecture (*ca.* 1140-1494) is not in spirit a world away from the classical. Yet Gothic

---

*It is noteworthy how much early French architecture rose in or near what had been Roman cities or Gallo-Roman sanctuaries: St.-Bertrand-de-Comminges, Arles, Lyon, Vézelay, Autun, Périgueux, Reims. And Notre-Dame-de-Paris was built (1163 and after) over the foundations of a Roman temple of Jupiter.

stained glass simply applied to walls the Roman technique of floor-mosaics, and the Gothic principle of taking stresses on external buttresses was already in use in Italy, in the Sanctuary of Fortune at Palestrina*, as early as 150 B.C.

Gothic castles derive from Byzantine versions of Roman camps, which French Crusaders had seen in the Holy Land. Thirteenth-century planned towns like Aigues-Mortes and Carcasonne† followed Roman models in their gridded street-plans. And the universities founded in the Gothic period, like Paris, *ca.* 1170, kept the Roman tradition alive; Pierre Abélard (1079-1142) lectured in Latin (at 5:30 in the morning!); François Villon (born *ca.* 1431) wrote love-poetry largely inspired by the Roman Ovid.

The Italian Renaissance, which saw a rebirth of classical architecture, came late to France, only after 1494, when Charles VIII began to imitate the Roman-inspired buildings he had seen in his invasion of Italy. At first, French architects simply laid a veneer, of Roman pilasters for example, on late mediaeval buildings. But under Francis I (1515-1547) it became *the* French style, and continued so until well into the nineteenth century. The Château de Chambord, on the Loire, has a Roman axial plan; the lovely bridge-gallery (1576) at Chenonceaux is inspired by Roman viaducts like the Pont-du-Gard. Francis' royal architect, Sebastiano Serlio, was an Italian, and from 1530 French architects began to go to Italy to study—as individuals, not, as later, under state subsidy. The result was a perfect spate of French classical buildings, of which the most famous is Fontainebleau (1528). The greatest lyric poet of the century, Pierre de Ronsard

---

Mute Stones Speak, Fig. 5.4.

†Carcasonne was restored in the nineteenth century by E. M. Viollet-le-Duc (1814-1879), who is chiefly famous (or notorious) as responsible for the Gothic revival (he restored Vézelay, Notre-Dame-de-Paris, and St.-Denis). But he was a first-rate Roman archaeologist as well, and Inspector of Ancient Buildings under Napoleon III.

(1524-1585) naturally went to the Greek Pindar and the Roman Horace for his inspiration.

Two Roman-inspired Paris squares, the charming Place des Vosges (1605), and the elegant Place Vendôme (1698), date from the seventeenth century. The same period saw a number of Renaissance-Roman planned towns rise in France, of which the best-known is Richelieu, with grid plan and uniform housing, founded by the famous cardinal. His, too, is the superbly restrained classical Palais-Royal in Paris (1629), and the purely classical Church of the Sorbonne (1635), planned with a Roman façade to face a Renaissance piazza. In the same tradition, with classical façades and Renaissance cupolas, are the ex-convent, now hospital, Val-de-Grâce (1645-60); Cardinal Mazarin's Collège des Quatre Nations, now the Institut de France, where the French Academy meets (1662); and St.-Louis-des-Invalides, (1680), where Napoleon is buried.

Formal French landscape architecture is also in the Roman tradition. In the mid-seventeenth century the great André Le Nôtre laid out near Paris the magnificent terraces of the Château de Vaux-le-Vicomte and St.-Germain-en-Laye, which go back to Roman Palestrina via the Renaissance architect Pirro Ligorio's terraced designs for Cardinal Ippolito d'Este's villa at Tivoli near Rome*. Le Nôtre also designed the stupendous two-mile vista of Louis XIV's palace gardens at Versailles (from 1669), which were in the mind of the Frenchman Pierre L'Enfant when he submitted designs for Washington, D. C. in 1791. At Versailles the massive buildings express an imperial absolutism as complete as that symbolized by the Roman Emperor Hadrian's vast villa near Tivoli.† The reign of Louis XIV was also the heyday of classicism in French literature: the tragedies of Corneille and Racine, inspired by the Greek Euripides and the Roman

*MSS 136, paperback 135.

†MSS 274-80, paperback 270-276.

Seneca, and the comedies of Molière, following the Romans Plautus and Terence.

So, even after Roman political and military influence ceased in the late fifth century, France has never ceased being Roman. The remainder of this chapter will be devoted to a somewhat more detailed account of the Roman-inspired architecture from the late seventeenth century onward which has made Paris today, by common consent, the most beautiful city in the world. This happy state of affairs is due in no small measure to creative imitation of Roman models by gifted French architects. This creative imitation did not come about by accident. It had four contributing causes: the founding of a school, the excavation of a site, the publication of a book, and the vanity of monarchs.

The school was the French Academy in Rome, founded by Louis XIV's minister J.-B. Colbert in 1666, and first opened to architects in 1720. For nearly two hundred years its fellows, winners in a stiff competion for the Prix de Rome, formed the aristocracy of French architects. They were exempt from military service, and they enjoyed the privilege of at least three years of study and travel abroad. They were required to submit measured drawings and restorations of ancient monuments, and it is therefore not surprising to see these reappear on the Paris scene: the Arch of Septimius Severus, Trajan's Column, Hadrian's Pantheon, and his temple of Venus and Rome. Their final task was to design a public building, according to a program sent down from Paris; as pensioners of the King, they were expected to show their gratitude by embellishing his capital. Winners of the Prix de Rome had a hand in the design, among the monuments to be discussed in this chapter, of the Arc de Triomphe du Carrousel, the Arc de Triomphe de l'Étoile, the Colonne Vendôme, the Madeleine, the Bibliothèque Ste.-Geneviève, Les Halles, and the Gare d'Orsay. Other buildings to which winners of the Prix contributed were the Odéon, the Palais-Royal, the theater of the Comédie Française, the Opéra, and the Invalides.

A second prime influence of French classicizing architecture, this time in décor, was the rediscovery in 1711 of the buried city of Pompeii, and its continuing excavation after that date. Frescoes from Pompeii and its sister city, Herculaneum, struck the fancy of eighteenth-century interior decorators. Their pattern-books, and the rooms they designed, are therefore full of Pompeian motifs like palmettes, grotesques, rosettes, swags, cornucopias, masks, candelabra, garlands, ivy, lions' heads, Bacchantes, Cupids, nymphs, genii, lyres, helmets, shields, swords, trophies, tripods, vases, dolphins, swans, griffins, and sphinxes, together with representations of mythological scenes like the centaur Chiron tutoring Achilles. Pompeian décor became the rage, not only for fireplaces, boudoirs, and bathrooms in private houses, but in cafés, restaurants, hotels (for example, the Ritz), pharmacies, and in the shops of confectioners, butchers, perfumers, armorers, modistes, tobacconists, and stationers. Pompeii profoundly influenced the styles called Louis XVI, Directoire, and Empire, and even the Egyptian motifs so popular under Napoleon owe at least as much to the Third Style at Pompeii as to the Little Corporal's campaigns on the Nile.

Of the many books which exerted an influence on French classicism, perhaps the most consequential was the Italian engraver G. B. Piranesi's *Prima parte di architettura* (1743), and the plates of Roman ruins in his *Antichità romane* (1748). His etchings, where pygmy men wander down colossal arcades, among enormous columns, past Cyclopean courses of stone, gave French architects a taste for the superhuman grandeur that was Rome. Piranesi knew the *pensionnaires* of the French School in Rome: they drew for him; he gave them advice. And they brought his huge folio volumes home to Paris, where stay-at-home architects could profit from them.

But perhaps the greatest stimulus to grandiosity in French classicizing architecture came from the megalomania of monarchs. Louis XIV commissioned the Porte St.-Denis to commemorate his victories on the Rhine; the Panthéon was begun in fulfillment of a vow made by Louis XV, and completed under his successor. Louis XVI also ordered the classicizing architect C.-N. Ledoux to build at the entrances to Paris a series of forty-seven customs-barriers, of which four survive. They were massive, Roman, and expensive, after the manner of the columned "follies" in ancient Roman pleasure gardens engraved by Piranesi, with ground plans cruciform, circular, square, triangular; replete with columns, pediments, cupolas, friezes, triglyphs, arches, caissoned vaults, arcades, consoles, pilasters, ramps—the whole vocabulary of ancient Roman architecture. Parisians were half amused and half exasperated at the grandeur of the buildings in which they were to be fleeced, and the expensiveness of Ledoux' projects created a scandal.

To Napoleon's thirst for glory we owe the Arch of the Carrousel, the Place Vendôme column, and the idea of the arch at L'Étoile and the Madeleine, neither of them finished till the reign of Louis-Philippe. Napoleon III's identification of himself with Julius Caesar and Augustus produced the whole boulevarded Roman city plan of Second Empire Paris, as worked out by the Baron Haussmann, together with Les Halles, the sewer system, and the Bois de Boulogne and de Vincennes.

During the nearly two hundred years in which classicism was the rule in French building, it dominated French literature as well. Two years after Blondel finished the Porte St.-Denis, Boileau published *L'Art poétique*. Both creative artists cherished the classical ideal of clear composition, common sense, nobility of style, and the creative imitation of classical models.

Near the other end of the period, Henri Labrouste finished his Bibliothèque Ste.-Geneviève (1850), in which a classical façade masks new structural materials, just seven years before Baudelaire published *Les fleurs du mal,* in which severe classical form expresses a romantic content. The Romantics preferred Greece to Rome (a symbol of the preference is the foundation of the

French School in Athens in 1846), and some of them preferred
Gothic to either. New materials (iron and glass) and some not
so new, like reinforced concrete, seemed to call for new methods
of treatment, and a new, democratic world of science and tech-
nology challenged the old humane, idealistic, aristocratic tradition. But the stamp that classicizing architects, after the high
Roman fashion, imposed upon Paris is with her still, and neither
she nor we are the losers by it, as the analysis of ten selected
examples will show.

Let us begin with a series of three triumphal arches. Louis XIV,
desiring to commemorate his war with Holland, commissioned the
architect François Blondel to build the Porte St.-Denis (1672;
Figs. 8.1 and 2), which stands an impressive seventy-nine feet
high. Its design is classical in its geometric simplicity: the height
of the single aperture of the arch is two-thirds the height of the
total structure to the cornice, and the width of the aperture is
one-third the total width of the arch; or, to put it another way,
the widths of each pier and of the opening of the arch are
equal. The south façade portrays in relief the Sun King's triumphant crossing of the Rhine (like Julius Caesar); the north, the
capture of Maestricht. The location of the arch was more important in the seventeenth century than it is today: the arch
spanned the route to the shrine of St. Denis north of the city, the
burial place of the Kings of France.

The idea of the Roman monumental arch was familiar to
seventeenth-century French architects. They had visited the arch
at Orange on their way to or from Italy (one of the earliest scientific studies of the monument was to be made by Caristie, win-
ner of the Prix de Rome in 1813), or they knew it from drawings.
The monument in Rome which the Porte St.-Denis most resembles, though the French version is on a larger scale, is the Arch of
Titus (Fig. 8.3), erected in A.D. 81 at the east end of the Roman
Forum. Like its French counterpart, it has but a single passage-

8.2   Paris, Porte St.-Denis

way, and it commemorates victories: of Titus over the Jews. Reliefs on the passageway portray on one side the triumphing general with the spoils of the Holy of Holies in Jerusalem, the

8.3   Rome, Arch of Titus

seven-branched candlestick, the table of the shewbread, and the
silver trumpets; on the other, Titus in a four-horse chariot,
crowned by Victory and escorted by lictors. In the seventeenth
century the arch was still encumbered by the Frangipani fortress,
not cleared away until 1822, but the reliefs were known, and may
well have inspired the brothers Anguier, who did the sculpture for
the Porte St.-Denis.

Our second arch, that of the Carrousel (Fig. 8.4) was commissioned by Napoleon to commemorate his victory at Austerlitz (1805). It stands in the Place du Carrousel, in front of the
site of the Tuileries Palace (destroyed in 1871), and was the
work of Napoleon's favorite architects, Fontaine and Percier,
who had won the Prix de Rome in successive years, 1785 and
1786. The model they chose to follow, at about two-thirds the
scale, was the Arch of Septimius Severus at the west end of the
Forum in Rome (Fig. 8.5). The reduced scale was imposed by

8.4   Paris, Arc du Carrousel

the size of the columns, which for economy were taken second-hand from depositories of used marble. The Carrousel arch, like the Roman original, uses marble of various colors and proveni-

8.5   Rome, Arch of Septimius Severus

ences, and has a main and two lateral passageways, flanked by the
second-hand columns, on pedestals. The columns, of the Composite order, support an attic divided into three fields by four
statues of soldiers in dress uniform; in the fields are inscriptions
dictated by Napoleon. Above the lateral arches, reliefs represent the battles of Ulm and Austerlitz, and the Peace of Tilsit;
above, and in the spandrels, Victories, trophies, and river gods;
in the center of the vault, the Emperor crowned by Victory. When
the arch was completed in 1808, it was crowned by the famous
bronze horses of San Marco, which Napoleon had removed from
Venice. They were returned after Waterloo, and replaced in
1828 by a modern bronze group representing the Restoration
driving a four-horse chariot. These details were a translation into
modern idiom of the décor of Severus' arch. It, too, had over its
side arches reliefs of victories won, at Seleucia and Ctesiphon on
the Tigris; it, too, had winged Victories and river gods in the

spandrels; and representations of victorious soldiers, but there are two differences: the soldiers are represented driving before them trousered Parthian captives, and they are placed on the pedestals supporting the columns, rather than in the attic above them, as in the Carrousel arch. Severus the North African, like Napoleon the Corsican, was an upstart; the grandiloquence of their arches reflects their latent inferiority complexes.

The third and most famous of Parisian monumental arches, the largest in the world—162 feet high, 147 feet wide—is the Arc de Triomphe de l'Étoile (Fig. 8.6), at the end of a grand perspective which leads the eye down the Champs-Elysées from the Arc du Carrousel. Though its cornerstone was laid under Napoleon, in 1806, it was not finished and dedicated until 1836, under Louis-Philippe. Its architect, J. F. T. Chalgrin, who had won the Prix de Rome in 1758, did not live to see his conception realized; he died in 1811. The effect of crispness and massiveness is enhanced by under-decoration, leaving great areas of unsculptured stone. The masterpiece is on the right pier facing the Champs-Elysées: the departure of the volunteers of 1792, commonly called "La Marseillaise," by F. Rude, who had won the Prix de Rome for sculpture in 1812. The six upper friezes depict Napoleonic victories and incidents of 1792 to 1805: the battle of Austerlitz appears again on the south face. Under the cornice a continuous frieze with hundreds of figures, larger than life, portrays the departure and glorious return of the French armies. Above the cornice, in metopes between triglyphs, shields bear the names of battles of the Napoleonic period. In the lateral arches, which, uniquely, run at right angles to the main passageway, are inscribed the names of hundreds of generals, with those who died in battle underlined. The Étoile arch, ever since its dedication, has had intimate associations with French military history. In 1840, Napoleon's remains, returned from St. Helena, passed under it. In 1919, the victorious armies of World War I marched through. On Armistice Day, 1920, the remains of France's Un-

8.6 Paris, Arc du Triomphe de l'Étoile

known Soldier were honored there; an eternal flame burns at the head of his simple grave. In 1944 a Paris freed at last from German occupation cheered General de Gaulle's passage. After his death, and after a typically French difference of opinion on the subject, the Place de l'Étoile was renamed for le Grand Charles.

The relation of the Étoile arch to earlier models is complex. Chalgrin is on record as having had in mind a doubling of the dimensions of the Porte St.-Denis, but the Étoile arch is also roughly double the size of the Arch of Constantine in Rome, which Chalgrin knew well. Besides, the years of gestation of the Étoile arch were a time in which much attention was being paid to the details of France's own Roman arch in Orange. Finally, by coincidence, the idea of carving upon a monumental arch the names of triumphing generals had also occurred to Augustus, who placed such a list upon his arch in the Roman Forum. At the time the Étoile arch was being planned and built, Augustus' list was known, but not its original position on his arch.

No modern tourist in Paris fails to visit the Panthéon, which dominates the Latin Quarter at what was once the east end of the Forum of the Roman city. The Panthéon was vowed as a church in 1744 by Louis XV in thanksgiving for recovery from an illness. Its architect, J. G. Soufflot, had not been a member of the charmed circle of winners of the Prix de Rome, but he had visited the Eternal City, and knew well Hadrian's Pantheon there, which inspired his design (Fig. 8.7) for the façade, pediment, and interior drum. The façade, with its huge, fluted Corinthian columns, also owes something to the Roman temple of Bacchus at Baalbek in the Lebanon; the swags in the frieze are borrowed from the tomb of Caecilia Metella in Rome, and the cupola from St. Peter's. Soufflot died in 1780; the building was not finished until 1789. Two years later, the anti-clericals of the Revolution deconsecrated it, using it instead as the repository of the bones of the great men of France. Among those represented in pedimental or other sculpture, or buried in the crypt, are Corneille, Lafayette, Voltaire, Rousseau, Diderot, Napoleon, Vercingetorix, Victor Hugo, Zola, and Soufflot himself. The contrast between the sever-

8.7   Paris, Panthéon

ity without and the richness within is also an effect sought and achieved by the Emperor-architect Hadrian in the Roman original. Within, Corinthian columns support frieze, cornice, and balustrade; the large central cupola is coffered, and supported by a mass of masonry, as in Hadrian's original; it also anticipated some of the buildings of the nineteenth century by being reinforced with iron.

The Pantheon in Rome, of about A.D. 125 (Fig. 8.8), is a massive concrete drum supporting a hemispherical cupola, an expression in architecture of a problem in solid geometry, to inscribe a sphere in a cylinder. It has perhaps been more imitated than any other ancient building, as a symbol of solidity and grandeur. Within, the drum is lightened by niches alternately semicircular and rectangular, and the heavy weight of the cupola is lightened

8.8   Rome, Pantheon

by coffering, which also reflects the lines of stress in the concrete. This controlled massiveness is what the architects of Soufflot's generation were after as they returned to the antique, and reconstructed a vision of ancient Rome through the engravings of Piranesi.

The reconstructed vision of the antique was not limited to Paris. Of all the provincial examples of Roman-inspired French architecture, perhaps the most interesting is one that never left the drawing board, the plan for a Rousseauistic ideal city at La Saline de Chaux, near Arc-et-Senans, designed between 1790 and 1795 by C.-N. Ledoux, the architect of the nortorious Paris customs-barriers already mentioned. Ledoux was the most imaginative, baroque, even surrealistic architect of his time; some of his projects are reminiscent of Piranesi's extraordinary *Prisons*. For the royal salt works at Arc-et-Senans he designed a circular garden city, of which a semicircle was actually built in 1775-1779. In the center of the perimeter was a Doric-porticoed gatehouse masking an artificial grotto; flanking it, in segments of the semicircle, workers' housing, with gardens behind. At what would have been the center of the planned circle rose, impressively temple-like, the director's house, flanked by the salt works themselves. This handsome ensemble was allowed to deteriorate, was heavily damaged by fire in 1918, and deliberately dynamited in 1926, thus depriving France of one of her major eighteenth-century monuments.

The other buildings of the model city, designed but never built, included, among others, a bridge over the River Loue, with piers in the shape of Roman triremes; a temple-like Bourse (anticipating the one in Paris, finished in 1815 by Brongniart, who failed the Prix de Rome three times); a square market, with an inner cruciform plan; domed public baths; a Pantheon-like church; a cemetery-columbarium, the central building of which was a sphere; a cannon foundry, square in plan, with pyramids at the corners like the Pyramid of Cestius in Rome; a hunting lodge on a terrace approached by ramps (like the Sanctuary of Fortune at Palestrina near Rome), its façades engraved with trophies like those on the arch at Orange; a Temple to the Glory of Women, with round corner towers, each reminiscent of Trajan's Column; a Maison d'Union, consecrated to the cult of moral values, and decorated with fasces; a cruciform boarding-school; and, most interesting of all, two buildings phallic in plan, a brothel or "Maison de Plaisir," and an "Oikema," or museum of vice (Fig. 8.9) where Ledoux professed the hope that the sexual display might by contrast lead those who had strayed back to the straight and narrow path of virtue. Both buildings appear to have been modeled after the Canopus of Hadrian's Villa at Tivoli (Fig. 8.10). In the Oikema, a central vestibule opens into parlors and semicircular galleries giving the plan a testicle-shape, and a penis-shaped corridor with rooms and baths opening off it leads to an elliptical salon. This phallic plan is perhaps a little perverse, since it would be wholly unnoticeable except from the air. This is an extreme example of eighteenth-century architectural symbolism, which supplied as it were "a system of musical keys that could be chosen according to a conventional code when designing different types of buildings." Architects have twice revolted against this conventionality within the last 100 years, once in Victorian Gothic—fortunately, because of the strength of the classical tradition, somewhat less endemic in France than in England or America—and again in the severe functionality of the Bauhaus style.

Hadrian's Canopus, which Ledoux probably knew in Piranesi's engraving, was a replica of a sanctuary in Alexandria, Egypt, where Hadrian's boy-love Antinous committed suicide in A.D. 130. The design of the deep terminal vault is unmistakably phallic.

Ledoux' fourfold imitation of Trajan's Column, mentioned above, is not the only one of its time. Between 1806 and 1810, in

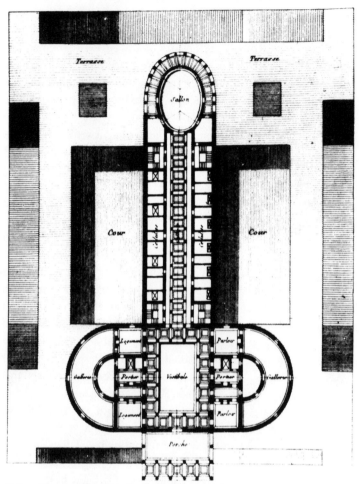

8.9   Chaux, *Oïkéma,* Ledoux plan

Paris, Napoleon's friends put up another, in the Place Vendôme.
Standing over 140 feet high, it was part of Napoleon's plan to
make Paris the most beautiful city in the world, but it is unfortunately out of scale with the exquisite seventeenth-century

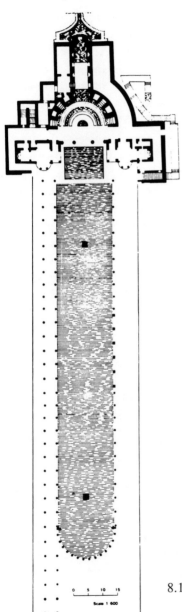

8.10   Tivoli, Hadrian's Villa,
       Canopus, plan

houses which surround the square. The Revolutionary government of France had at one time entertained the notion of moving
Trajan's Column bodily from Rome and re-erecting it in Paris.
Mercifully, this vandalism never took place. Indeed, the architect J. Gondoin—second Prix de Rome, 1758—was commissioned to design a new column in bronze over a masonry core;
the bronze was melted down from 1,200 cannon captured at
Austerlitz. The feats of Napoleon's armies between the years
1805 and 1807 were recorded on the column, spirally, in seventy-
six reliefs. The masonry base was adorned with trophies, like the
the original in Rome. On the summit stood a statue of Napoleon
in the costume of Julius Caesar. This suffered vicissitudes. The
royalists took it down in 1814 and replaced it with a huge Bourbon fleur-de-lis. Louis-Philippe replaced this symbol in 1833 with
a statue of Napoleon in contemporary uniform, which now adorns
the façade of the church of the Invalides; the mobs of the Com-
mune threw the column down in 1871; when the Third Republic
restored it, in 1874, it was surmounted by a copy of the original
statue, in Roman costume (Figs. 8.11-12).

The original, erected by the Senate and people of Rome in A.D.
113, is built of eighteen drums of Parian marble, and stands a
little less than 125 feet high, over fifteen feet shorter than the
Napoleonic version. The base, adorned with trophies and an inscription, contained Trajan's ashes in a golden urn. Above, in
a spiral over 650 feet long, was unrolled, in over 2,500 figures,
the saga of Trajan's two campaigns (A.D. 101/2 and 105/6)
against the Dacians (the modern Romanians). The reliefs supply a treasure house of information on the details of Roman
warfare and native folkways. In the sixteenth century François
I of France had casts made, now in the St.-Germain-en-Laye museum. In the eighteenth, Percier, who was to become Napoleon's
favorite architect, had himself suspended in a basket on the
column, and made careful drawings of the subject matter of the
scrolls. A gilt-bronze statue of Trajan surmounted the column.

8.11   Paris, Colonne Vendôme

It was lost in the Middle Ages, and Pope Sixtus V replaced it in 1588 with the present statue of St. Peter. It is possible by special permission to climb the column, by a spiral staircase of 185 steps, and enjoy, from the platform below the statue, a splendid view of Rome. The column as a whole expresses the affection of the Roman people for the ruler they called "the best of princes"; the Parisian version hardly evokes such universal applause.

8.12   Rome, Trajan's Column

Another example of Napoleon's megalomania, expressed in
Roman architectural terms, was the Temple de la Gloire he conceived in 1806, which was finally consecrated as the church of the
Madeleine in 1842. Its Roman model is commonly said to be the
Maison Carrée at Nimes multiplied by four, but in grandiosity
the Madeleine more closely resembles Hadrian's Temple of
Venus and Rome (Figs. 8.13-14), opposite the Coliseum in
Rome, which actually exceeds it in size (Roman temple, 475 by
328 feet; Madeleine, 354 by 141 feet). Napoleon's choice as
architect was Pierre Vignon, the pupil, executor, and perhaps the
natural son of Ledoux. When Vignon died in 1828, he was buried
in the fifty-two-columned peristyle of the temple he had designed,
and his work was carried on by J. J. M. Huvé (Prix de Rome,
1770). Vignon designed the façade of the Madeleine, on its lofty
Roman podium, twenty-eight steps high, with its eight sixty-five-

foot Corinthian columns, to match the 1808 façade of the Palais Bourbon at the other end of the vista through the Place de la Concorde, and across the Seine.* Vignon designed the Madeleine

with an apsidal end, as in Hadrian's temple, and three cupolas, supported by Roman vaulting, and concealed in the exterior view by a pedimental roof with skylights: all the light comes from above. Huvé's interior, with its polychrome marble paneling, Corinthian columns, Ravenna-like mosaics, and coffering in the cupolas, resembles in grandeur Michelangelo's church of Santa Maria degli Angeli in Rome, which was a Renaissance enrichment of a part of the baths of Diocletian (A.D. 305). The Madeleine's great bronze doors, nearly thirty-five feet high, might well be a rendition at double scale of the doors of Diocletian's Senate House in Rome, now in re-use at St. John Lateran. At various times during its long building history, the Madeleine was destined for a variety of secular uses: as a Stock Exchange, a library, an assembly chamber, a law court, the Bank of France, the Opera; it narrowly missed being a railway station. What mattered was not function but symbol: Roman massiveness and richness would buttress equally well the claims to solidity and trustworthiness of financial, intellectual, political, legal, artistic, or religious life. The architects who had been dazzled in the Eternal City by the marble, the porphyry, the jasper, the gilded vistas, the mosaics, the frescoes, returned to reproduce in Napoleonic France the might and majesty of Imperial Rome.

The most probable Roman model for the Madeleine, Hadrian's temple of Venus and Rome, set in a peristyle of sixty-six columns, was two temples with apses back to back, a colossal architectural

---

*The Palais Bourbon was conceived as the Temple of Law, as the Madeleine was the Temple of Glory. Delacroix painted (1839-45) famous classical themes and figures for its library; the Roman ones include Rome's legendary King Numa, holding nocturnal congress with the nymph Egeria; Cicero fulminating against the villainous governor Verres; the poet Ovid exiled among the Goths; the Roman Stoic philosopher Seneca, paired with Socrates; and the Roman encyclopaedist Pliny the Elder.

8.13   Paris, Madeleine

8.14   Rome, temple of Venus and Rome,
        reconstruction-drawing

pun, for Venus in Latin is AMOR, and AMOR is ROMA spelled backwards. The façades had ten columns to the Madeleine's eight (and the Maison Carrée's six), the interior gleamed with red porphyry columns; the roof was covered with gilt tiles. Hadrian's temple, like Napoleon's, was embellished in a later reign. In all cases, the monarchs, ancient and modern, were free to propagandize their own glory, untrammeled by any financial limitations.

The Bourbon Restoration (1815-1830), and the July Monarchy (1830-1848), added little to French classicizing architecture, except the completion of buildings planned earlier. But Napoleon's nephew Louis-Napoleon, later Napoleon III, identified himself, as we saw in Chapter 2, with Caesar and Augustus, and wished to rival his uncle in leaving his stamp upon Paris, in using Roman-inspired buildings as a backdrop to his imperial pageant. In this endeavor he had the efficient and even ruthless cooperation of his prefect, the Baron Georges Haussmann, another Alsatian, like Colonel Stoffel, who had helped him with excavations of Caesarian sites. In seventeen years (1853-1870) Haussmann changed the face of Paris, well aware of the precedent he was following in Roman city planning. His boulevards, with long straight vistas toward some impressive monument, had antecedents in such Roman colonies as Orange. The opening to the public of the two Bois, de Boulogne and de Vincennes—"the lungs of Paris," Haussmann called them—has Roman parallels: Caesar and Agrippa bequeathed their gardens to the people of Rome; the Gardens of Sallust on the Pincian Hill, though they remained imperial property, were open to the public; Vespasian diverted the vast grounds of Nero's Golden House to public use. (Haussmann's vastly increased number of public urinals were soon nicknamed "Vespasiennes".) Haussmann proudly referred to his great extension of the Parisian sewer system as his "Cloaca Maxima," after the famous sewers in Rome.

Meanwhile, new materials were enabling architects to design

buildings in which form followed function, as the exploitation of concrete, from about 80 B.C., had enabled Roman architects to do. A carpenters' strike in 1840 turned architects' attention to the possibilities of iron, but such was the strength of the classical tradition that down to the end of the nineteenth century iron-frame buildings generally continued to have Roman façades and details. Thus, though Henri Labrouste (Prix de Rome, 1824) used iron in the framework of his Bibliothèque Ste.-Geneviève (1843-1850), he gave it a classical façade (Figs. 8.15-16), to blend with the Panthéon opposite. This façade ultimately derived, via Renaissance *palazzi,* from fireproof warehouses of about A.D. 100 in ancient Rome's port town of Ostia. In the reading room of Labrouste's library, a central row of cast-iron fluted columns, slim in scale like those in Pompeian wall paintings, supports two barrel vaults on exposed iron arches whose serpentine openwork is a Roman decorative detail. On the exterior, the nineteen bays of arches, with swags below and palmettes above, produce a façade described by Henry-Russell Hitchcock as "outrank[ing] in distinction almost all other examples of Renaissance Revival anywhere in the world"; and that revival is a Roman—or Ostian—one.

The Ostia warehouse of Epagathus, like Labrouste's library, is both functional and severely decorative. It is functional in the sense that its material, brick-faced concrete, is completely fireproof; it is decorative in its use of unadorned brick, in the relieving arches, and especially in the doorway, where an arch is flanked by engaged Ionic columns supporting a pediment with dentils. The warehouse was not excavated until 1922, but ancient Roman apartment houses very similar in design and décor had been known to architects since the fifteenth century. Thus the Ostia architect, like Labrouste, used the conventional décor of his period to give beauty to an essentially utilitarian building.

Labrouste's success with the Bibliothèque Ste.-Geneviève led to his being commissioned to build the vast reading room (1862-

8.15 Paris, Bibliothèque Ste.-Geneviève

8.16 Ostia, warehouse of Epagathus, doorway

1868) of the Bibliothèque Nationale. Here sixteen thirty-two-foot slim cast-iron columns support nine cupolas, in exposed cast-iron and glazed tile; the lighting, as in Hadrian's Pantheon, is entirely from above, through "eyes" in the cupolas. Classical details of décor include cameo-like medallions, and a pair of Caryatids (Greek maidens) supporting the arch behind the delivery desk. The Caryatid motif was borrowed from the Erechtheum in Athens, but we now know that Hadrian had imitated them in a portico surrounding his pool in front of the Canopus temple.

Napoleon III and Haussmann, in the Roman tradition, wanted history to record that they had contributed to the utility as well as to the beauty of their city. They therefore commissioned a Central Market—Les Halles Centrales—built between 1851 and 1858 by Victor Baltard (Prix de Rome, 1833). His design has been called a Vitruvian basilica in iron and glass. Vitruvius' *De architectura,* written before 27 B.C., became the Bible of Renaissance architects, and was still influential among Rome-trained architects of nineteenth-century France. The basilica of Fano in Italy, which Vitruvius himself built and described, took what became canonical form, with a high nave, lower side aisles, and lighting through clerestory windows. Trajan's architect designed such a basilica in vaulted concrete for the market adjoining his Forum (Figs. 8.17-18).

Baltard designed for Les Halles a series of ten pavilions, in pairs; the six pairs of the eastern section cover 545 by 407 feet. Each had a long nave. Iron columns with classical capitals supported arches, which gave access to the side aisles, containing the market stalls. The ground floor arches supported the glassed-in clerestory, with twice the number of arches, half as wide. The nave, which provided a covered access road, was roofed by a combination of arches and trusses, both of iron, and left visible. Like a good Roman, Baltard embellished his frieze with palmettes. In modern Paris, Les Halles cause monstrous traffic jams,

8.17 Paris, Les Halles Centrales

8.18 Rome, basilica in Trajan's market

and are to be dismantled; their passing will leave a gap in the history of nineteenth-century French architecture as serious as that caused for the eighteenth by the destruction of Ledoux' masterpiece at Arc-et-Senans. In Les Halles, Roman engineering devices were combined with Roman architectural décor to provide, with new materials, a classical functional solution for a modern need.

The basilica of Trajan's market, which was known in the sixteenth century and then lost to view until 1929/30, has six concrete cross vaults in the nave, six market stalls on each side, and clerestory lighting, with an access road, the Via Biberatica, at the side. It was a government building, for the distribution of the dole to the poor. Its architect used concrete as functionally as Baltard used glass and iron.

In designing Les Halles, Baltard had profited from the experience since 1835 of the builders of Parisian railway stations, who had, like the builders of ancient Roman baths, to solve the problem of roofing vast spaces. As Roman engineer-architects used the vault in concrete, so the nineteenth-century French used the vault in iron and glass. Our final example is the Gare d'Orsay (now called the Gare d'Orléans), built between 1898 and 1900 by V. Laloux (Prix de Rome about 1871). An example of a Roman solution is the "Temple of Diana" at Nimes (Figs. 8.19-20). By the time Laloux had finished, the Second Empire was thirty years in its grave; in 1870, Haussmann was dismissed and his master deposed; the Third Republic was no more remarkable for its architecture than for its statesmen. And so Laloux' façade for the Gare d'Orsay seems over-decorated; its inspiration flags. The French classical tradition is in decadence. His façade presents heavy double-pilaster-framed arches with surrounds of "rusticated" blocks, set with deep-sunk joints, and lions' heads above the keystones. Huge statues weigh down the cornice. In the pavilions at the ends, the arches are superimposed, with huge

8.19   Paris, Gare d'Orsay, train-shed

clocks in the upper ones. Obelisks, like those the Romans used to decorate their circuses, surmount the pavilion roofs. The interior is somewhat more successful, because of the comparative restraint of the glass-and-coffered vault. But the vault has no function. In the older stations, it served to dissipate smoke; in the Gare d'Orsay, the trains were electrified, and came in on the lower level, so that the vaulted train shed serves only for ticket windows and newspaper kiosks: it is ostentatious, not functional. By comparison with this, the quiet tastefulness of the "Temple of Diana," already described in Chapter 3, is refreshing.

The classical style in French architecture, whose creative vital-

8.20   Nimes, "Temple of Diana"

ity petered out with the end of the nineteenth century, had for
seven generations given dignity, harmony, and beauty to the
French and Parisian scene. Whatever symbolism an architect

desired or was directed to express, the creative imitation of a Roman monument would express it. In triumphal arches or a sculptured column, a Sun King or a Corsican corporal could bask in reflected Roman glory. A Roman building connoted grandeur and solidity, whether for religious or secular purposes: the Panthéon and the Madeleine served both. Or the might and majesty of the Roman Empire might be borrowed to express the would-be might and majesty of the French State Railways, as in the Gare d'Orsay. Even sexual symbolism might be expressed, as Ledoux proved in his drawings for Chaux, with full Roman confidence that concrete could be used to enclose space in any shape. And as in Roman buildings, so in classicizing French, a sense of function was not absent, as Labrouste's libraries and Baltard's Halles magisterially prove.

The classical style, as we saw, suited an age which at its best was humane, idealistic, aristocratic, and universal. The new, *fin de siècle* age was scientific, realist, bourgeois, and nationalistic, and its buildings reflected the difference. The new, unadorned, glass-box, international style does not suit all tastes, and does not fit a historic city like Paris. But some of its practitioners have worked recently in Roman material, reinforced concrete, with dazzling results. The Centre des industries et des techniques (CNIT), finished in 1958, is by three winners of the Prix de Rome, and is the world's largest concrete vault, resting on only three supports. The techniques of Roman engineers made it possible. And one of its architects collaborated with a Hungarian-American, and with Pierluigi Nervi, a modern Roman engineer-architect, on the UNESCO building in Paris, also completed in 1958, and symbolizing man's aspirations toward a world which shall be, as the Roman Empire was in its prime, educationally, scientifically, culturally one. The frame of the UNESCO building was one of the landmarks of concrete construction in Europe, but its façade, like Laloux' for the Gare d'Orsay, is unfortunate. Its interior décor, on the other hand, is the work of the finest con-

temporary artists, including Picasso. Nervi's trapezoidal concrete conference hall is superb. In these masterpieces the genius of
Roman architect-engineers comes to life again.

And so we come to the end of our archaeological survey of pre-
Roman and Roman France, which has covered, with gaps, nearly
14,500 years, from the cave-paintings of Lascaux to the Picasso
of UNESCO. We have looked at Breton megaliths, Greek colonies, and Gallic oppida; seen Caesar conquer and Augustus con-
solidate; watched Gaul prosper, in town and countryside, in the
security of the Roman peace. We have observed how tolerantly
the Roman allowed the Gaul, so long as he kept that peace, to
worship his own gods in his own way. We have traced how the
best Gallic craftsmen, without losing touch with their native roots,
adapted and adopted Roman techniques: Caesar remarks on the
ingenuity of the Gallic race, quick to borrow and develop any
idea suggested to it by others. We have, finally, applied this gen-
eralization to French architects since the seventeenth century,
who by creative imitation of Roman originals made Paris into
what many regard as the most beautiful city in the western world.
The story, since it involves, on both the Gallic and the Roman
side, frail, passionate, and imperfect human beings, has not been
one of uninterrupted progress; there have been dark and tragic
moments, which this chronicle has not tried to gloss over. But if
the modern Frenchman feels, as he does, that he is the most
urbane and civilized man on the face of the earth, he can justify
this feeling with the thought that for over five hundred years he
harbored Romans in his land.

Chronology

B.C.

12,500	Lascaux: cave-paintings
2970±200	Fontaines-Salées: wells
ca. 1400	Carnac: menhirs
ca. 1000	Fontaines-Salées: cremation necropolis
7th c.–49 B.C.	St.-Blaise: Greek walled settlement
ca. 600	Marseille founded by Phocean Greeks
ca. 550	Ensérune, Gallic *oppidum*, founded
late 6th c.	Vix: bronze *crater*
6th-5th c.	Glanum (St. Rémy) founded by Greeks
late 5th c.	Ensérune II: stone houses, polygonal wall
5th-2nd c.	Roquepertuse: Gallic sanctuary
4th-3rd c.	Fontaines-Salées: earthworks, chariot road
ca. 400–250	Ensérune necropolis
390	Rome sacked by Gauls
3rd c.	Glanum I: Hellenistic buildings
ca. 225	Ensérune III: Roman influence begins
218	Hannibal crosses Rhone en route to Italy
3rd-2nd c.	Olbia (Hyères) flourishes
	Roquepertuse: statue of heroized chief
123	Entremont: Gallic *oppidum* captured by Romans
118	Narbonne (Narbo Martius) founded; capital of new Roman province
102	Aquae Sextiae (Aix): Romans defeat Teutons
after 101	Glanum II: Roman buildings
100	Julius Caesar born
76-74	Fonteius governor of Gallia Narbonensis
72	Lugdunum Convenarum (St.-Bertrand-de-Comminges) founded by Pompey
61	Aedui ask Rome for aid against Suebi
58-50	**Caesar** proconsul in Gaul
58	Caesar halts Helvetii; routs Ariovistus
57	Attacks Belgae

247

56	Fights naval battle against Veneti
53	Campaigns in northeast Gaul
52	Vercingetorix elected Gallic leader at Bibracte
	Caesar besieges Avaricum (Bourges)
	Caesar defeated at Gergovia
	Labienus victorious at Paris
51	Caesar defeats Vercingetorix at Alesia
	Camp at Nointel
50	Caesar captures Uxellodunum (Puy d'Issolu)
49	Marseille and St.-Blaise fall to Caesar (Civil War)
46	Rome: Caesar celebrates Gallic triumph
	Arles: Roman colony
	Narbonne: settlement of veterans of Tenth Legion
43	Lyon: colony of Plancus
	Vienne: colony of Mark Antony
ca. 40	St.-Rémy: mausoleum of Julii
36	Arausio (Orange) founded: colony for
	Second Legion
ca. 30	Forum Julii (Fréjus) founded: naval colony
27–A.D. 14	**Augustus**

Augustan buildings and monuments, not precisely dated:

	Arles: theater and cryptoporticus
	Lyon: Forum
	Vienne: Temple of Rome and Augustus
	Orange: theater
	Chiragan: villa, phase I
25	St-Bertrand: trophy
24	Aleria founded: colony on Corsica
ca. 20	Glanum: Agrippan basilica; Temple of Valetudo
	St.-Rémy: arch
20-19	Nimes: Tour Magne; Maison Carrée
	Pont du Gard, aqueduct
	Vernègues: Temple of Jupiter
16-14	Lyon: theater, phase I
after 14	Cimiez: amphitheater
12	Lyon: Altar of the Twelve Gods, dedicated by
	Drusus

12 or 7	Autun founded: Aedui moved down from Bibracte
10	Lyon: Claudius, future Emperor, born
9-7	Glanum: Temples of Gaius and Lucius Caesar; theater
6	La Turbie: trophy

A.D.

1st c., not precisely dated:

Vaison-la-Romaine: House of Messii; Portico of Pompey

Paris: arena

Bouray: bronze god

Lezoux: Mercury

Fontaines-Salées: Temple; baths, phase I

Neuvy-en-Sullias: bronzes

14-37	**Tiberius**

Tiberian, not precisely dated:

Mavilly: reliefs

Paris: reliefs of Esus and Tarvos Trigaranus

before 19	Saintes, arch
19	Lyon: amphitheater, phase I
20-21	Vaison: theater
ca. 26	Orange and Carpentras: arches

41-54	**Claudius**

Claudian, not precisely dated:

Allonnes: precinct of Mars

St.-Germain-Sources-Seine: water sanctuary

Montbouy: water-sanctuary

Chassenon: water-sanctuary

42	Vienne: Temple of Rome and Augustus rededicated to Augustus and Livia
42	Boulogne founded, as base for first successful invasion of Britain
ca. 49	Saintes: amphitheater
ca. 50	Montmaurin: villa rustica
	Paris: rue Gay-Lussac baths
after 54	Haut-Bécherel: Mars sanctuary

54-68	**Nero**
	Neronian, not precisely dated:
	Autun: Temple "of Janus"
	Puy-de-Dôme: peak-sanctuary of Mercury
	Marseille: wall of Crinas
before 68	Arles and Nimes: amphitheaters
69-79	**Vespasian**
	Vespasianic, not precisely dated:
	Fréjus: amphitheater
	Autun: theater, phase I
	Alesia: theater
before 79	Vaison: House of the Silver Bust
81-96	**Domitian**
	Domitianic, not precisely dated:
	La-Motte-du-Ciar: Vulcan sanctuary
	Glanum: triumphal monument
before *ca.* 85	La Graufesenque: potteries flourish
after *ca.* 85	Lezoux: potteries flourish
ca. 93	Domitian decrees uprooting of half Gallic vines
1st-2nd c.	Berthouville: silver treasure
	Gallo-Roman glass, phase I
98-117	**Trajan**
	Trajanic, not precisely dated:
	St.-Bertrand flourishes
	Chiragan villa, phase II
	Paris: Forum
103	Autun: theater, phase I
ca. 112	Alesia: basilica
117-138	**Hadrian**
	Hadrianic, not precisely dated:
	Nimes: "Temple of Diana"
	Périgueux: Tour de Vésone
	Sanxay: Temple of Apollo; baths, phase I; amphitheater
	Fontaines-Salées: baths, phase II
ca. 119	Lyon: theater, phase II
	Lyon: amphitheater, phase II

138-161	**Antoninus Pius**

Antonine dynasty (138-192), monuments not precisely dated:

	Chassenon: water sanctuary flourishes
	Reims: kit of ophthalmologist C. Firmius Severus
ca. 150	Alesia: Forum
	Vienne: Theater of Mysteries
	St.-Bertrand: basilica shops
	Bavai: cryptoporticus
	Moulin-du-Fâ: Mars sanctuary
	Villards-d'Héria: Mars sanctuary
150-200	Chiragan: villa, phase III
	Reims: cryptoporticus
160	Lyon: temple of Cybele; Odeon
161-180	**Marcus Aurelius**
165-190	Buzenol: relief of mechanical reaper
ca. 167	Besançon made a colony: Porte Noire
ca. 175	Châtelard-de-Lardiers: peak-sanctuary of Mercury destroyed
175-225	Paris: Collège de France baths
177	Lyon: persecution of Christians; St. Blandina martyred
180-192	**Commodus**
186	Maternus' marauders: Fontaines-Salées baths, phase III
2nd c.	Reims: cryptoporticus
	Donon: peak-temple of Mercury; Jupiter-giant column
193-211	**Septimius Severus**
193-423	Gallo-Roman glass, phase II
198-217	**Caracalla**
	Grand: Temple of Apollo; basilica; demi-amphitheater
2nd-3rd c.	Cimiez: baths
	Reims: Porte de Mars
	Paris: Cluny baths
	Essarois: water-sanctuary
Early 3rd c.	Paris: arena destroyed; Ile de la Cité rampart
	Fréjus: Baths (Porte Dorée)

ca. 210	Tertullian comments on fertility of Gaul
228-235	**Alexander Severus**
	Alesia: House of the Silenus destroyed
ca. 250-276	Montmaurin: villa, phase II
ca. 256-274	Jublains: post-station
270-274	**Tetricus** Emperor in Gaul
276	Widespread barbarian destruction; *e.g.,* Bavai; Montmaurin II; Berthouville Mercury sanctuary, phase I
after 276	Bavai: reduced perimeter
276-282	**Probus** encourages wine-making
285-337	**Constantine I**
	Chassenon water sanctuary in disuse
before 300	Sens: reliefs of artisans
4th c.	Chiragan: villa, phase IV
312	First literary mention of Burgundy wine
324-361	**Constantine II**
	Fontaines-Salées: baths, phase IV
ca. 350	Montmaurin: villa, phase III
351-361	Allonnes: Mars sanctuary destroyed
ca. 360	Lyon: barbarians cut aqueducts
364-375	**Valentinian I**
ca. 371	Ausonius praises Moselle and Bordeaux wines
383-388	**Maximus**
	St.-Germain-Sources-Seine: water-sanctuary destroyed
	Chiragan: villa destroyed
408	St.-Bertrand, Chiragan villa, and (probably) Fontaines-Salées destroyed by Vandals
440	Salvian comments on fertility of Aquitania
460-465	Lac Aydat: villa of Sidonius Apollinaris flourishes

Modern Names of Roman Settlements

Modern	Roman
Aix en Provence	Aquae Sextiae
Aleria	Colonia . . . Aleria
Arles	Arelate Sextanorum
Autun	Augustodunum
Bavai	Bagacum
Besançon	Vesontio
Bordeaux	Burdigala
Boulogne	Gesoriacum
Bourges	Avaricum
Carpentras	Carpentorate
Cimiez	Cemenelum
Fréjus	Forum Julii
Jublains	Noviodunum
Limoges	Augustoritum
Lyon	Lugdunum
Mt. Beuvray	Bibracte
Narbonne	Narbo Martius
Nimes	Nemausus
Orange	Colonia . . . Arausio
Orléans	Cenabum
Paris	Lutetia Parisiorum
Périgueux	Vesunna Petruciorum
Puy-d'Issolu	Uxellodunum
Reims	Durocortorum
Saintes	Mediolanum Santonum
St.-Bertrand-de-Comminges	Lugdunum Convenarum
St. Rémy	Glanum
Sens	Agedincum
Vaison-la-Romaine	Vasio
Vienne	Colonia . . . Vienna

Sources of Illustrations

(See also Foreword)

Grenoble, B. Arthaud: 6.10
New York, S.P.A.D.E.M.: 1.10; 4.8
Paris
    Archives photographiques: 1.2, 6, 7; 2.3, 11, 12; 4.16; 5, 10, 11; 6.5, 7; 7.5, 12; 8.2
    Ina Bandy: 2.2; 8.6
    Documentation photographique: 7.8
    Giraudon: 1.13; 2.6; 6.12; 7.15
    Photothèque française: 2.9; 4.9; 5.12; 6.9
    Touring Club: 1.11, 12; 4.7, 10, 11, 12; 7.11
    R. Viollet: 1.8; 4.5, 19; 5.8; 7.13
Rome, Fototeca: 8.8, 10, 18
St.-Germain-en-Laye, Musée historique: 1.14; 6.2, 3; 7.2
Toulouse, Yan: 5.4, 5

All other photographs are either by the author or assumed to be in the public domain.

Books and Articles Consulted

Abbreviations

ArchJ: Archaeological Journal
BEFAR: Bibliothèque des Ecoles Françaises d'Athènes et de Rome
BEHE: Bibliothèque de l'Ecole des Hautes Etudes
CollLat: Collection Latomus
CRAI: Comptes rendus de l'Académie des inscriptions et belles lettres
G: Gallia
GSupp: Gallia, Supplément
Manuel: A Grenier, *Manuel d'archéologie gallo-romaine,* 4 vols. (Paris 1931–1960)
MemAcInscr: Mémoires presentés par divers savants à l'Académie des inscriptions et belles lettres
MHF: Monuments historiques de la France
RA: Revue archéologique
RAECE: Revue archéologique de l'est et centre-est
Receuil: E. Espérandieu-R. Lantier, *Receuil général des bas-reliefs, statues, et bustes de la Gaule romaine,* 14 vols. (Paris 1907–1955)
(Unless otherwise indicated, Paris is the place of publication.)

1. Before the Romans

F. BENOIT, "Résultats historiques des fouilles d'Entremont, 1946–67," *G* 26 (1968) 1–31

——, *Entremont* (Aix-en-Provence 1957)

——, *Recherches sur l'hellénisation du Midi de la Gaule* (Aix 1965)

G. BIBBY, *The Testimony of the Spade* (New York 1956)

F. CHAMOUX, "Les Antiques de St.-Rémy-de-Provence," *Phoibos* 6/7 (1951/3, publ. 1955) 97–111

M. CLERC, *Aquae Sextiae* (Aix-en-Provence 1916)

——. *Massilia: histoire de Marseille dans l'antiquité,* 2 vols. (Marseille 1927)

J. COUPRY, "Fouilles à Olbia," *G* 12 (1954) 3–33

G. DANIEL, *Lascaux and Carnac* (London 1955)

——, *The Megalith Builders of Western Europe* (London 1958)

Y.-M. FROIDERAUX, "Aménagement des grottes de Lascaux," *MHF* n.s. 1 (1955) 97–105

H. DE GERIN-RICARD, *Le sanctuaire préromain de Roquepertuse* (Marseille 1927)

P. R. GIOT, *Brittany* (*Ancient Peoples and Places* series, London 1960)

J. HAWKES, *Prehistory and the Beginnings of Civilization* (London 1963)

J. JANNORAY, "Ensérune," 2 vols., *BEFAR* 181 (1955)

R. JOFFROY, "Le trésor de Vix," *Monuments Piot* 48 (1954) 1–68

R. LANTIER, "Le sanctuaire de Roquepertuse," *Archäologischer Anzeiger* 1929, 281–292

A. LEROI-GOURHAN, *Treasures of Prehistoric Art* (New York 1967)

H. ROLLAND, "Fouilles de Glanum", *GSupp* 1 (1946); 11 (1958); *G* 25 (1967) 407; *Revue archéologique de Narbonnaise* 1 (1968) 93–99; *GSupp* 21 (1969); "Le mausolée de Glanum". *GSupp* 21 (1969)

——, *Fouilles de St.-Blaise* (Martigues 1967)

2. Caesar Slept Here

P. BAUME, P.-F. FOURNIER, *Gergovie* (Clermont-Ferrand 1962)

O. BROGAN, N. L. SHADWELL, "Gergovia," *Antiquity* 10 (1936) 210–217

——, E. DESFORGES, "Gergovia," *ArchJ* 97 (1940) 1–36

——, *Roman Gaul* (London 1953)

J. BULLIOT, *Fouilles de Mt. Beuvray de 1867 à 1895,* 2 vols. (Autun 1899)

CAESAR, *Bellum Gallicum,* ed. L.-A. Constans, 2 vols. (1937)

J. CARCOPINO, *Alésia et les ruses de César* (1958)

CICERO, *Pro Fonteio,* ed. A. Boulanger (1950)

L.-A. CONSTANS, *Guide illustré des campagnes de César* (1929)

P.-M. DUVAL, *Paris antique* (1961)

————, "Alésia et les Gaulois," *Archeologia* no. 24 (Sept.–Oct. 1968) 6–13

M. GORCE, *César devant Gergovie* (Tunis-Paris 1942)

A. GRENIER, *Manuel* 1 (1931) 187–225: camps; 3.1 (1955) 128–142: Narbonne

J. HARMAND, *Une campagne césarienne: Alésia* (1967)

J.-J. HATT, *Histoire de la Gaule romaine*² (1966)

P. HÉLÉNA, *Les origines de Norbonne* (Toulouse-Paris 1937)

J. JOLY, *Guide du siège d'Alésia* (Dijon 1966)

C. JULLIAN, *Histoire de la Gaule* 3 (1909)

————, *Vercingetorix*, new. ed. by P.-M. Duval (1964)

J. LE GALL, *Alésia, archéologie et histoire* (1963)

G. MARTHERAT, "Les ponts-de-fascines de Jules-César à Breuil-le-Sec (Oise)", *RA* 1936 53–94

————, "La technique des ponts-de-fascines de César," *ib.* 1937, 38–62

NAPOLEON III, *Historie de Jules-César*, 2 vols. (1865–1867)

T. RICE HOLMES, *Caesar's Conquest of Gaul*² (Oxford 1911)

J. TOUTAIN, "Le véritable caractère de la Gaule romaine," *Receuil de la société des antiquaires de France, 150ᵉ anniversaire* (1955), unpaged

R. E. M. WHEELER, K. M. RICHARDSON, *Hill Forts of Northern France* (Oxford 1957)

3. *Augustan Cities*

Anon., *A la recherche de Vienne gallo-romaine* (Vienne 1965)

A. AUDIN, *Lyon, miroir de Rome dans les Gaules* (1965)

J.-C. BALTY, "Etudes sur la Maison Carrée de Nimes," *CollLat* 47 (1960)

F. BENOIT, "Le sanctuaire d'Auguste et les cryptoportiques d'Arles," *RA* 39 (1952) 31–67

————, "Le developpement de la colonie d'Arles et la centuriation de la Crau," *CRAI* (1964) 156–169

————, "Les fouilles de Cimiez," *CRAI* (1962) 207–219. See also *id, G* 22 (1964) 600–607; and M. M. Euzetinat, *ib.* 25 (1967) 429–433

G. CHARLES-PICARD, "Les trophées romains," *BEFAR* 187 1957): on La Turbie

L.-A. CONSTANS, *Arles antique* (1921)

A. DONNADIEU, *La Pompéi de la Provence: Fréjus* (1927)

P.-M. DUVAL, "Rapport préliminaire sur les fouilles de Cemenelum (Cimiez, 1943)," *G* 4 (1946) 77–136

E. ESPÉRANDIEU, *Le Pont du Gard et l'aqueduc de Nimes* (1926)
————, *La Maison Carrée à Nimes* (1929)
————, *L'amphithéâtre de Nimes* (1933)

H.-P. EYDOUX, "Les cryptoportiques d'Arles," *Monuments et trésors de la Gaule* (1958) 186–202
————, "Les vestiges de Fréjus," *Résurrection de la Gaule* (1961) 189–221

P. A. FÉVRIER, "Forum Iulii (Fréjus)," *Itinéraires ligures* 13 (Cuneo 1963)

J. FORMIGÉ, *Le théâtre romain de Vienne* (1931)
————, "La trophée des Alpes," *GSupp* 2 (1940)

A. GRENIER, *Manuel* 3.1 & 2 (1958); 4 (1960)

J. GUEY, A. AUDIN, "L'amphithéâtre des Trois Gaules à Lyon," *G* 20 (1962) 117–145; 21 (1963) 125–164; 22 (1964) 37–61

J. JEHASSE, "Les fouilles d'Aleria: l'acropole et ses problèmes," *G* 21 (1963) 77–109

M. LOUISE, A. BLANCHET, *Carte archéologique de la Gaule romaine* 8 (1941): Nimes, Pont du Gard

R. NAUMANN, "Der Quellbezirk von Nimes," *Denkmäler antiker Architektur* 4 (Berlin 1937)

A. PELLETIER, "Les fouilles du 'Temple de Cybèle' à Vienne (Isère). Rapport provisoire" *RA* (1966) 113–150. See also *G* 26 (1968) 580-583 (St.-Romain-en-Gal mosaic)

M. RAMBAUD, "L'origine militaire de la colonie de Lugdunum," *CRAI* (1964) 252–277

P. VARÈNE, "La Tour Magne, Nimes (Gard),' *8ème Congrès international d'archéologie classique* (1963) 643–652

P. WUILLEUMIER, "Fouilles de Fourvière à Lyon" *GSupp* 4 (1951)
————, *Lyon, métropole des Gaules* (1953)

4. The Fruits of Romanization

R. AMY, P. M. DUVAL, J. FORMIGÉ J. J. HATT, A. PIGANIOL, C. PICARD, G. C. PICARD, "L'arc d'Orange," *GSupp* 15 (1962)

P. BARRIÈRE, *Vessuna Petruciorum* (Périgueux 1930). See also *G* 21 (1963) 514–525

L. CHÂTELAIN, "Les monuments romains d'Orange," *BEHE, Sciences historiques et philologiques* 170 (1908)

C. DANGIBEAUD, *Saintes, Mediolanum Santonum* (Saintes, 1933)

P.-M. DUVAL, "Les galeries souterraines du Forum de Reims," *G* 12 (1954) 97–99

H.-P. EYDOUX, "La Résurrection de Lugdunum Convenarum," *Lumières sur la Gaule* (1960) 157–189

———, "Reims et les vestiges de sa splendeur antique," *Hommes et dieux de la Gaule* (1961) 117–144

C. FOHLEN, ed., *Histoire de Besançon* 1 (1964), 60–69: "La porte noire," by L. Lérat

A. GRENIER, *Manuel* 1 (1931) 568–569 (Saintes, bridge); 3 (1958) 650–657 (Saintes, amphitheater); 1.337–45; 3.234–44, 458–463, 799–803 (Autun); 440–447 (Périgueux); 1.564–567 (Porte de Mars, Reims)

E. HUBERT, "Servitude et grandeur de l'archéologie," *Archeologia* no. 3 (Mar.–Apr. 1965) 73–77 (Saintes bridge)

R. LIZOP, *Les Convenae et les Consoranni* (Toulouse-Paris 1931)

P. PELLERIN, *En ressuscitant Vaison-la-Romaine* (1962)

C. PICARD, "Observations sur les statues de prisonniers et les trophées de St.-Bertrand-de-Comminges," *CRAI* (1933) 138-159

G. C. PICARD, "Sur la composition et la date des trophées de St. Bertrand-de-Comminges," *ib.* (1942) 8–17

———, "Trophées d'Auguste à Lugdunum Convenarum," *Mémoires de la Société archéologique du Midi* 21 (1947), unpaged

A. PIGANIOL, "Les documents cadastraux de la colonie romaine d'Orange," *GSupp* 16 (1962)

B. SAPÈNE, *St.-Bertrand-de-Comminges (Lugdunum Convernarum), centre touristique de l'art et d'histoire* (Toulouse 1954)

———, "L'amphithéâtre de Lugdunum Convenarum," *Revue de Comminges* 70 (1957) 97–111

————, "Une récente résurrection dans les fouilles romaines de St.-Bertrand-de-Comminges," *ib.* 64 (1951) 3–15

J. SAUTEL, *Vaison dans l'antiquité*, 3 vols., with supplements (Avignon-Lyon 1927–42)

————, *Sites, histoire et monuments de Vaison-la-Romaine* (Lyon 1955)

H. STERN, "Le cycle des mois de la Porte de Mars à Reims," "Hommages Grenier," *CollLat* 58 (1962), 3 vols., 1441–1446

E. THÉVENOT, *Autun cité romaine et chrétienne* (Autun 1932)

5. *Country Houses and Late-Empire Cities*

H. BIÉVELET, "L'exploration archéologique de Bavai," *Revue du Nord* 46 (1964) 183–206

A. BLANCHET, *Les enceintes romaines de la Gaule* (1907)

R. M. BUTLER, "Late Roman Town Walls of Gaul," *ArchJ* 116 (1959) 25–50

P.-M. DUVAL, "Une enquête sur les enceintes gauloises," *G* 17 (1959) 37–62

————, *Paris antique* (1961)

H.-P. EYDOUX, "La fasteuse villa de Montmaurin," *Monuments et trésors de la Gaule* (1958) 220–252

————, "L'ensemble monumental de Bavai," *ib.* 80–102

————, "Un département-pilote de l'archéologie aérienne: la Somme," *Les terrassiers de l'histoire* (1960) 19–50

G. FOUET, "La villa gallo-romaine de Montmaurin," *GSupp* 20 (1969) *G* 20 (1962), Index, s.v. *Villa*

A. GRENIER, "Habitations gauloises et villas romaines dans la Cité des Mediomatrices," *BEHE* 157 (1906) 54–92, 122–174

————, *Manuel* 2 (1934) 782–941 (villas, esp. Chiragan); 1.454–63 (Jublains); 4 (1960) 544–550 (Montmaurin)

L. JOULIN, "Les établissements gallo-romains de la plaine de Martres-Tolosanes," *MemAcInscr*, 1. série, 11 (1901): Chiragan.

E. LAURIN, *Les ruines gallo-romaines de Jublains* (Laval 1928)

P. MAC KENDRICK, "The Romans and the Land," *The Roman Mind at Work* (Princeton 1958) 65–69, 158–163

SIDONIUS APOLLINARIS, *Epistles* 2.2 (on his villa)

J. SOYER, "Découverte d'emplacements d'habitat gallo-romain dans la plaine d'Aix," *Revue archéologique de Narbonnaise* 1 (1968) 201–218

VITRUVIUS, *De architectura* 6.6 (on farmhouses)

E. WILL, *Bavai, cité gallo-romaine* (Lille-Douai 1957)

6. Shrines and Statues

E. BABELON, *Le trésor d'argenterie de Berthouville* (1916)

P. BARRIÈRE, "Une bourgade gallo-romaine: Chassenon, ses monuments et ses puits," *Revue des études anciennes* 39 (1937) 241–255

F. BENOIT, *Art et dieux de la Gaule* (1969)

R. BILLORET, "La Basilique de la ville antique de Grand," *CRAI* 1965, 63–74

P.-M. DUVAL, *Les Dieux de la Gaule* (1957)

H.-P. EYDOUX, "Le temple d'Allonnes", *Résurrection de la Gaule* (1961) 311–332

———, "Les thermes de Fontaines-Salées," *Monuments et trésors de la Gaule* (1958) 103–123

———, "Prospections de la région de Sens," *ib.* 88–99

———, "Les découvertes de Chassenon," *Résurrection de la Gaule* (1961) 251–278

J. FORMIGÉ, "Le sanctuaire de Sanxay," *G* 2 (1944) 43–97

A. GRENIER, *Les Gaulois*[2] (1945)

———, *Manuel* 3.210–5 (Vernègues); 424–433 (Puy-de-Dôme); 452–457 (Moulin-du-Fâ); 487–490 (Grand); 939–943 (Sanxay); 4.323–6 (Allonnes); 449–460 (Fontaines-Salées); 527–528 (Châtelard); 553–567 (Sanxay); 572–577 (Chassenon); 608–639 (St.-Germain-Sources-Seine); 672–680 (Villards d'Héria); 721–724 (La Motte du Ciar); 730–733 (Montbouy); 768–777 (Berthouville); 803–811 (Bécherel); 829–840 (Donon); 904–909 (Grand)

B. LACROIX, "Un sanctuaire de l'eau de plan circulaire aux Fontaines-Salées," *RAECE* 14 (1963) 81–114

P. LAMBRECHTS, *Contribution à l'étude des divinités celtiques* (Bruges 1942)

F. LE ROUX, *Les Druides* (1961)

R. LOUIS, "L'exploration archéologique de Vézelay gallo-romain: les thermes de Fontaines-Salées," *MHF* 3 (1938) 65–75

R. MARTIN, "Sculptures en bois découvertes aux Sources de la Seine," *RAECE* 14 (1963) 1–19

P. MONCEAUX, "Le grand temple de Puy-de-Dôme, le Mercure gaulois, et l'histoire des Arvernes," *Revue historique* 35 (1887) 225–262; 36 (1888) 1–28, 242–278

Receuil, Nos. 1589, 1609, 2067, 2403, 2970, 3134, 3412, 3653, 4569–4603, 4767–8, 4894, 4898; vol. 9, p. 280; vol. 11, p. 21; vol. 12, p. 23; 8337

E. SALIN, "Aperçu général de la ville antique de Grand," *CRAI* (1965) 75–86

E. THÉVENOT, "Sur les traces des Mars celtiques," *Dissertationes archaeologicae Gandenses* 3 (Bruges 1955)

——, *Divinités et sanctuaires de la Gaule* (1968)

J. DE VRIES, *La Religion des Celtes* (1963)

J. ZWICKER, *Fontes religionis Celticae*, 3 vols. (Berlin 1934)

7. Gallic Arts and Crafts

A. ALBENQUE, *Les Rutènes* (Rodez 1948)

——, "Nouvelles fouilles à La Graufesenque," *RA* 37 (1951) 175–191

F. BENOIT, "Le moulin hydraulique de Barbegal," *Arts et livres en Provence* 33 (1957) 48–51. See also *RA* 6 sér., 15 (1940) 19–80

A. BLANCHET, *Etude sur la décoration des édifices de la Gaule romaine* (1913)

L. BOUSQUET, *Six leçons d'histoire de Rouergue* (Rodez 1942)

Bulletin du comité archéologique de Lezoux 1 (1968): La céramique

R. DION, *Histoire de la vigne et du vin en France* (1959)

M.-A. DOLLFUS, "Les instruments d'ophthalmique chez les gallo-romains," *Archives d'ophthalomogie* 18 (1958) 633–651

————, "L'exercice de l'ophthalmologie à l'époque gallo-romaine," *Bulletin de la Société Nationale des Antiquaires de France* (1963) 107–124

P.-M. DUVAL, *La vie quotidienne en Gaule* (1952)

H.-P. EYDOUX, "Un trésor mystérieux: les bronzes d'art de Neuvy-en-Sullias," *Réalités et énigmes de la Gaule*[2] (1965) 197–221

————, "Le Rouergue antique," *Les Terrassiers de l'histoire* (1966) 195–229

————, L'agriculture perfectionée des gallo-romains," *L'histoire arrachée de la terre* (1962) 145–160

————, "Une usine-pilote gallo-romaine: la meunerie hydraulique de Barbegal," *Monuments et trésors de la Gaule* (1958) 203–219

C. FABRE, "Les industries céramiques de Lezoux," *RA* 6 sér. 5 (1935) 91–110

G 19 (1961) 322–324: iron-smelting furnaces, Allogny (Cher)

A. GRENIER, *Manuel* 4.727–9 (Neuvy-en-Sullias); 2.942–1017 (quarries and mines)

————, "La Gaule romaine," in T. Frank, *Economic Survey of Ancient Rome* 3 (Baltimore 1937) 379–664

F. HERMET, *La Graufesenque*, 2 vols. (1934)

B. HOFFMAN, *L'évolution de la céramique sigillée en Gaule romaine* (Brussels 1961)

E. KRETZSCHMER, *Bilddokumente römischer Technik* (Düsseldorf 1967)

J. LASSUS, "Réflexions sur la technique de la mosaïque," in *Conférences-visites du Musée St. Gsell* (Algiers 1957) 5–42

L. MAURIN, "Etablissement vinicole à Allas-les-Mines (Dordogne)," *G* 22 (1964) 209–221

MORIN-JEAN, *La Verrerie en Gaule sous l'empire romain* (1913) *Receuil*, Nos. 2767, 2769, 2978, 2984, 3232, 3608, 3677, 2681, 3685

M. RENARD, "Technique et agriculture en pays trévire et rémois," *CollLat* 38 (1959)

J.A. STANFIELD, G. SIMPSON, *Central Gaulish Potters* (Oxford 1958)

J.R. TERRISSE, "Les céramiques sigillées gallo-remains des Martres-de-Veyre," *GSupp* 19 (1968)

K.D. WHITE, *Agricultural Implements of the Roman World* (Cambridge 1967)

8. Roman-Inspired Architecture in Modern France

A. BLUNT, "Art and Architecture in France, 1500–1700," *Pelican History of Art* (Baltimore 1953)

B. CHAMPIGNEULLE, *Paris de Napoléon à nos jours* (1969)

P. COLLINS, *Changing Ideals in Modern Architecture, 1750–1950* (Montreal 1965)

G. GROMORT, *Essai sur la théorie de l'architecture* (1946)
Guide bleu: Paris (1934)

L. HAUTECOEUR, *Histoire de l'architecture classique en France*, vols. 4–7 (1952–1957)

H.-R. HITCHCOCK, "Architecture, 19th and 20th Centuries,"[2] *Pelican History of Art* (Baltimore 1963)

G.E. KIDDER SMITH, *The New Architecture of Europe* (New York, 1961)

P. LAVEDAN, *French Architecture* (Harmondsworth 1956)

G. LUGLI, *Roma antica: il centro monumentale* (Rome 1946)

P. MAC KENDRICK, *The Mute Stones Speak* (New York 1960; paperback 1966)

E. NASH, L. CURTIS, A. NAWRATH, *Das antike Rom*[3] (Vienna-Munich 1957)

———, *Pictorial Dictionary of Ancient Rome*, 2 vols. (London 1961)

D.H. PINKNEY, *Napoleon III and the Rebuilding of Paris* (Princeton 1958)

S.B. PLATNER, T. ASHBY, *A Topographical Dictionary of Ancient Rome* (Oxford 1929)

M. RAVAL, J.-CH. MOREUX, *Claude-Nicolas Ledoux* (1945)

MARQUIS DE ROCHEGUDE, *Guide pratique à travers le vieux Paris* (1923)

Index